GENDER, SEX AND GOSSIP IN AMBRIDGE

GENDER, SEX AND GOSSIP IN AMBRIDGE: WOMEN IN THE ARCHERS

Edited by

DR CARA COURAGE

DR NICOLA HEADLAM

United Kingdom – North America – Japan – India
Malaysia – China

Emerald Publishing Limited
Howard House, Wagon Lane, Bingley BD16 1WA, UK

First edition 2019

Copyright © 2019 Emerald Publishing Limited

Reprints and permissions service
Contact: permissions@emeraldinsight.com

No part of this book may be reproduced, stored in a retrieval
system, transmitted in any form or by any means electronic,
mechanical, photocopying, recording or otherwise without
either the prior written permission of the publisher or a licence
permitting restricted copying issued in the UK by The Copyright
Licensing Agency and in the USA by The Copyright Clearance
Center. Any opinions expressed in the chapters are those of
the authors. Whilst Emerald makes every effort to ensure the
quality and accuracy of its content, Emerald makes no
representation implied or otherwise, as to the chapters'
suitability and application and disclaims any warranties,
express or implied, to their use.

British Library Cataloguing in Publication Data
A catalogue record for this book is available from the British Library

ISBN: 978-1-78769-948-9 (Print)
ISBN: 978-1-78769-945-8 (Online)
ISBN: 978-1-78769-947-2 (Epub)

ISOQAR certified
Management System,
awarded to Emerald
for adherence to
Environmental
standard
ISO 14001:2004.

Certificate Number 1985
ISO 14001

INVESTOR IN PEOPLE

CONTENTS

About the Editors   *vii*

About the Authors   *ix*

Acknowledgements   *xv*

Preface
Nicola Headlam and Cara Courage   1

Section One – Inside Ambridge   9

1. In Conversation with Alison Hindell
    Nicola Headlam and Cara Courage   11

2. 'I'm Not One to Gossip': Roots, Rumour and Mental
    Well-being in Ambridge
    Charlotte Connor, aka Charlotte Martin, and Susan Carter,
    actor, in BBC Radio 4's The Archers   21

Section Two – Women's Talk: Informal Information
Networks that Sustain the Village   35

3. Neighbourhood Watch: Gossip, Power and the
    Working-class Matriarch in *The Archers*
    Claire Mortimer   37

4. In Praise of Gossip – Why Tongue-wagging and the
    Rumour Mill Are Important in Ambridge
    Louise Gillies   49

5. 'Almost Without Exception They Are Shown in Their
    Relation to Men': Ambridge Women and Their Conversations
    Sarah Kate Merry   63

6. Foucault, Freda Fry and the Power of Silent Characters
     on the Radio
     Rebecca Wood   77

Section Three – Gendered Expectations: Within the Home   87

7. 'This Isn't About Curry, Alistair': Shula Hebden Lloyd
     and Iris Murdoch on Love

     Hannah Marije Altorf   89

8. Oh Baby! Unplanned Pregnancy and A Woman's Right to
     Choose
     Carolynne Henshaw   101

9. Women's Work?: Civil Society Networks for Social
     Stability or Social Change in Ambridge
     Nicola Headlam   115

10. Strong or Silenced? The Under-representation of Mental
      Health Problems in Ambridge's Women

      Elizabeth Campion   131

Section Four – Gendered Expectations: Beyond the Home   141

11. 'What Would the Neighbours Say?': Gender and
      Sexuality Diversity in *The Archers*
      William Pitt   143

12. Ambridge: Keeping the Pipeline of UK Female Scientists
      Flowing
      Jane Turner and Clare Warren   153

13. I Am Woman Hear Me Roar – And Now Watch Me
      Play Cricket
      Katharine Hoskyn   167

14. Sow's Ears and Silk Purses: Upcycling and *The Archers*
      Madeleine Lefebvre   179

Index of Ambridge Residents   193

Index   197

ABOUT THE EDITORS

Dr Cara Courage

Dr Cara Courage is Head of Tate Exchange, UK, the Tate's platform dedicated to socially engaged art, and an arts, society and place curator, researcher, writer and practitioner. Cara has a 20-year career in the arts, specialising in arts in the public realm and public engagement with the built environment, active across all art forms in this and working as a consultant and project manager for public and private initiatives, as well as having her own placemaking practice. As well as co-editing two volumes of Academic Archers books (2016 & 2017) Cara is author of *Arts in Place: The Arts, the Urban and Social Practice* (2017) and the co-editor of *Creative Placemaking: Research, Theory and Practice* (2018).

Dr Nicola Headlam

Dr Nicola Headlam is the Head of the Northern Powerhouse within the Cities and Local Growth Unit and is on secondment from her research fellowship at The University of Oxford. Prior to that she spent several years as the Urban Transformations and Foresight Future of Cities Knowledge Exchange Research Fellow funded by the ESRC. She is primarily interested in knowledge mobilisation for urban transformations. She has worked for 20 years on issues relating to the translation of research into policy and is an adaptable urbanist, media commentator and author. Her expertise is in comparative city governance, economic development, regeneration and urban policy and the networks that enable human flourishing, including the role of public agencies in place, specifically sub-national spatial and urban policy, and the role of leadership and partnerships. Nicola is passionate about the role of universities in public policy and practice and is a founding member of the Urbanista UK network for women involved in positive urban change.

She goes to Ambridge every evening to escape all that.

ABOUT THE AUTHORS

Hannah Marije Altorf

Hannah Marije Altorf is a Reader in philosophy at St. Mary's University, Strawberry Hill, London, where she was programme director for eight years. She has written on the philosophical work of Iris Murdoch and on different forms of philosophical dialogue. Together with Mariëtte Willemsen she translated *The Sovereignty of Good* into Dutch and presented a fictional dialogue between Murdoch, Bayley and two friends at its presentation. She is presently working on a short introduction to Murdoch's philosophical work.

Elizabeth Campion

Elizabeth has returned to the University of Cambridge to complete an Master of Laws in 2018–2019, having previously worked in two City law firms. She was a proud participant in the 2018 Academic Archers conference.

Charlotte Martin (aka Dr Charlotte Connor)

Charlotte is an actor and research psychologist. She trained and worked as a dancer before attending drama school at The Old Rep, Birmingham. In 1982 she was cast as 'Susan Carter' in BBC Radio 4's *The Archers*, a character which she plays to the present day. She continues to work in theatre, television, radio and as a voice-over artist, but has also gone on to pursue an academic career, studying psychology at the University of Birmingham and achieving a PhD in 2008, exploring the role of power and expressed emotion in depression in people with auditory hallucinations. Her current academic role is focussed specifically on early identification and intervention in youth mental health, working in collaboration with schools and communities. Recent studies have included improving care pathways for young people with psychosis, and screening for early warning signs of eating disorders in young people in schools. She has published 15 academic papers and regularly presents at academic conferences worldwide. Charlotte is also a keen Tweeter (@ambridgeview) and regularly tweets during the Sunday *Archers Omnibus Tweetalong*.

Louise Gillies

Louise Gillies is a clinical academic, working as both a social scientist and a genetic counsellor. Her main research areas are family communication (particularly relating to inherited disease), use of genograms to explore family issues and genealogy and family health history. The goings on in *The Archers* have provided a great source of practise material at both masters counselling level and PhD family studies. *The Archers* has been in her life for about the same length of time as her current relationship (a couple of decades). Eleven years in, she decided she was too old to have a boyfriend and informed Mr G that they were going to get married the following year. He didn't say no, which obviously meant yes (this has been a subject of much debate since the wedding). She hopes that Fallon and Harrison (at the time of writing) have a boringly normal (and happy) marriage.

Carolynne Henshaw

Carolynne Henshaw is most decidedly not an academic, but is a long-time nightly listener of *The Archers*. She has worked for a UK pregnancy services provider and a charity offering support to women faced with abnormal pregnancy screening results. She is pro-choice.

Katharine Hoskyn

Katharine Hoskyn spent her childhood and part of her adult life in Britain and now lives in New Zealand. She is currently teaching on contract with the Auckland University of Technology, after teaching marketing and advertising for 20 years and supervising students on work placement. She has an undergraduate degree in social sciences, a graduate diploma in business and an MPhil on the use of sports events to encourage sport participation. Her doctoral research investigates the membership of community sports clubs. Her current research blends social science and marketing, with a focus on community issues. She has been listening to *The Archers* on and off since 1968.

Madeleine Lefebvre

Madeleine Lefebvre is Chief Librarian of Ryerson University in Toronto, Canada. Born in the UK, she holds an MA from Edinburgh University as well as MA and MLS degrees from the University of Alberta. She is a Fellow of the UK Chartered Institute of Library and Information Professionals and an Associate of the Australian Library and Information Association. Her book, *The Romance of Libraries*, was published by Scarecrow Press in 2005. In 2015 Madeleine was appointed a trustee of the Niagara-on-the-Lake Public Library and is passionate about the role public libraries play in the community.

Sarah Kate Merry

Dr Sarah Kate Merry is a knitter, a Radio 4 addict, and a Research Associate in the Centre for Postdigital Cultures at Coventry University. Her PhD is in information studies and her personal research interests include how the Internet has changed friendship and the value of non-participatory membership of online communities. However, her actual work involves research into improving support for students with disabilities in Latin America and North Africa, open education in the Middle East and the benefits of board games for people who are socially isolated. Sarah was indoctrinated into *The Archers* at an early age and despite several attempts has never quite managed to leave.

Claire Mortimer

Claire Mortimer is a film historian, writer and teacher. She completed her PhD in 2017 at the University of East Anglia, her research being concerned with ageing women and British film comedy. She has published and presented at conferences on a range of ageing women, including Margaret Rutherford and Peggy Mount.

William Pitt

William 'Bill' Pitt is a social researcher based in a world leading research agency in London. He works across a range of policy areas and has an interest in gender and sexuality. He's a mixed methods practitioner who is passionate about data agnostic research and using evidence to advocate for social change. An avid fan of *The Archers*, Bill has listened daily for (almost) a third of his life. He holds a BA in anthropology and psychology from the University of Sydney, Australia, and an advanced certificate in market and social research practice from the Market Research Society in London.

Jane Turner

Associate Professor Jane Turner works in the School of Education at the University of Hertfordshire. She is a primary teacher educator, author and consultant, and director of the national Primary Science Quality Mark. As a newly qualified teacher in 1986, she was introduced by a colleague to the delights of the Sunday morning omnibus.

Clare Warren

Clare Warren has worked as a primary school teacher, teacher educator and education consultant. She is studying for a PhD in primary science education at the University of Hertfordshire. Clare became familiar with *The Archers* as a child when every Sunday morning the kitchen was filled with the smell of baking and the sounds of Ambridge.

Rebecca Wood

Rebecca is an ESRC Postdoctoral Fellow at King's College, London, and an Honorary Research Fellow at the University of Birmingham. She is a former languages teacher who subsequently specialised in autism education. Rebecca completed her PhD at the Autism Centre for Education and Research at the University of Birmingham where she was supported by a full-time scholarship. She was also project manager of the Transform Autism Education project, a tri-national scheme funded by the European Commission. Rebecca has a particular interest in language and communication and has applied some of the ideas from this area of study to *The Archers*, of which she is a devoted listener.

ACKNOWLEDGEMENTS

With thanks for all of our contributors, our community of Academic Archers, the team at Emerald and Oxford Publicity Partnership, and to the people of Ambridge, the women in particular, for proving year on year to be such a fascinating subject of study.

PREFACE

Nicola Headlam and Cara Courage

WHAT ARE THE WOMEN OF AMBRIDGE TELLING US?

Whilst *The Archers* is the butt of many a joke, whilst there is much comedy and in-jokes laced through the scripts and whilst we at Academic Archers pay close attention to the humour in and to be had from the lives of those in Ambridge, the women of Ambridge are our site of serious study. This book collects papers across a wide spectrum of social, political, economic and cultural issues through which we use *The Archers* lens to interrogate the lives of the women in the programme and how far their voices support or challenge tropes of feminist or post-feminist lives. Of course, *The Archers* is scripted and carefully plotted in order to reflect societal norms, and our authors herein take varied routes in questioning how far women are in charge of their own destinies in Ambridge and in comparison to what we see in the lives of women outside of Borsetshire. What then are the women of Ambridge telling us? What can they tell us of the prevailing structures of a society which has been structurally patriarchal? Of internalised

1

gendered socialisation and the roles thereof, and intersectional identity formation?[1]

Informed by feminist, critical race theories and critical disability studies, we view *The Archers* as of huge and essentially contested sociocultural significance. In exploring the many threads of gender and feminist or anti-feminist themes in *The Archers*, in this book we call attention to how far individual identity and gendered roles and norms are presented in Ambridge. As is appropriate we focus in our second section on *Women's Talk*; it has been observed that the informal networks of women's talk and gossip networks have been sites of power and resistance when men are in charge of more formal arenas. In the third section, *Gendered Expectations: Within the Home*, we focus on the gendered implications of the home, where there are reproductive choices and decisions around love and marriage as well as the emotional labour of family life. The fourth, *Gendered Expectations: Beyond the Home*, focusses on gendered implications beyond the home as women participate in the workforce.

ATTENTION TO POWER DYNAMICS IN *THE ARCHERS*

Gendered tropes are not hard to find in *The Archers*. In his celebrated BBC Radio 4 *John Finnemore's Souvenir Programme*, the titular comedian creates a pastiche of Ambridgian gender characterisations that is recognisable to even the occasional listener of *The Archers*. The men 'always sound

---

[1] In broad terms, gender identity is how a person views themselves with respect to masculinity or femininity and how this view of the self leads to the enactment of, or resistance to, socially ascribed gender roles. Gender roles dictate what is considered acceptable for men and women in terms of behaviour, career, parenting, style of dress and so on (Chicago Unbound).

tired' from their hard work of farming business; the 'insuf-
ferably wry women' are the incidental makers of coffee, speak
to move the plot along and are smugly tolerating of the
menfolk (BBC Radio 4a).

The form of *The Archers* presents a more or less equal
number of male and female characters, but there has been
unease that the gender stereotyping on display is of an
unhelpful kind. In her contribution to the Women of
Ambridge Panel at the 2018 Academic Archers conference,
Charlotte Martin (actor, Susan Carter) aka Dr Charlotte
Connor (Research Psychologist, Warwick University) caused
gasps from the auditorium by pointing out that there were no
women writers of *The Archers* until 1975 coinciding with a
period where the future of *The Archers* was far from certain as
it made the transition from post-war farming propaganda
towards contemporary drama in a rural setting (see Chapter
2). This is hard to imagine given the subsequent revered status
of Vanessa Whitburn as the programme's long-running editor.
Often accused of simultaneous 'Brooksidisation' of Ambridge
(she had worked on the Channel 4 soap) and of shifting the
focus to the lives of the women, hitherto 'farmers' wives', in a
career retrospective, Whitburn admitted that she arrived as an
ambitious editor, ready to make her mark with a controversial
first storyline: Elizabeth Archer's abortion. She was stung by
the early pejorative portrayal of her as a domineering, feminist
editor with an eye only on the big stories. It is not hard to find
outrage and opprobrium from those who feel that gendered
agendas abound in *The Archers*, but it can also do no right.
On the one hand, it is perceived by some to be written by
those of the 'liberal metropolitan elite', admonished for being
part of a 'political correctness gone mad'.

On the other hand, however, it simultaneously lacks
feminist role models, and often pointedly, career women are
conspicuous by their absence. Critics claim that Whitburn

turned a gentle, snoozy countryside tale into a soap (the term loaded with class derision) abundant with crime, sex, drugs, abortion, homosexuality, biracial marriage and families, wayward teenagers, adultery, single motherhood, donated sperm and IVF – in short, everything of everyday life through time that however upsets some listeners' aspic-set bucolic image of rural life.

However, whilst the listeners might not be settled in a view on how far the women of Ambridge are feminist (or not) or of the veracity gender identities and roles available to them, there is an important point of method to explain. Ambridge is a socially constructed place – made by the scriptwriters and by the actors, and by us as listeners. We view *The Archers* as a 'polysemic' text, that being, one in which listeners can construct their own meanings instead of passively adopting the preferred or dominant, themes – and in doing so, assert their own power in the listener subject position. As the real-time backchannel of *The Archers* Tweetalong highlights, there are myriad interpretations of storylines, characterisations and actions, informed by the listeners' own intersectional[2] lived experience, leading to divergent interpretations of the same thing. In the context of Ambridge too of course, multiple disadvantage collects around gender, socioeconomic status, housing status, and of either being childless or able to afford childcare. The intersection of these natal, social and politico-economic factors keeps Emma scraping glitter from her gussets (being unable to afford to replace clothes washed with a vial of glitter so having to make do until it would eventually wash out) whilst the middle-class characters thrive from their comparative wealth and consequent purchasing power of

---

[2] 'The theory that the overlap of social identities contributes to the specific type of oppression and discrimination experienced by an individual' (Dictionary.com).

being able to afford replacement clothes if the same laundry day mishap happened to them.

WHAT ARE OUR AMBRIDGOLISTS TELLING US?

We are honoured to open this book with an *Inside Ambridge* section, with contributions from two *Archers* heavyweights: an 'in conversation' with former acting editor, Alison Hindell, and a chapter from the most Academic Archer of us all, Dr Charlotte Connor, aka Charlotte Martin, actor, Susan Carter in BBC Radio 4 *The Archers*. Hindell is able to share her insights into the making of *The Archers* and the impact this has on the women of Ambridge and her thoughts on how some of the key storylines both developed and are developing. Connor spoke at the 2018 Academic Archers conference in reflection on the papers in the *Women in Ambridge* session, informed by her perspective as one of *The Archers* cast, her deep knowledge and love of her character and her academic specialism as a research psychologist. Her chapter goes deeper into these aspects and offers us listeners (and now readers) a consideration of the ambivalence often felt towards Susan, her power and agency in Ambridge located though her role as 'the gossip' and into the mental health and support networks in the village.

We move on in the second section, *Women's Talk: Informal Information Networks that Sustain the Village*, the contributors reclaim women's conversation as a core resource in a system where they may not have access to other forms of capital: agreeing with Connor preceding, Susan is not to be sidelined as a gossip, but rather her active interest in the lives of others gives her the function of the Greek chorus commentary on dramatic action. Starting with Claire Mortimer, *Neighbourhood Watch: Gossip, Power and the*

Working-Class Matriarch in The Archers. Louise Gillies continues with *In Praise of Gossip – Why Tongue-Wagging and the Rumour Mill Are Important in Ambridge,* asserting that gossip is in fact not just imperative for us listeners, as a means of communicating action to us (thank you Susan and Lynda), but how in small communities it can foster a sense of belonging, is a form of learning and maintains social order. Turning to the conversations that Ambridge women have with each other, Sarah Kate Merry, *'Almost Without Exception They Are Shown in Their Relation to Men': Ambridge Women and Their Conversations,* takes a statistical approach to what women say and who they say it with to understand what this says of their power positions and dynamics. This section closes with a consideration of the woman we never heard from, but was a locus of village life and *The Archers* storylines, in *Foucault, Freda Fry and the Power of Silent Characters on the Radio,* from Rebecca Wood. Silent characters from literature and television are brought into our frame, and as with the use of music in *The Archers,* the non-verbal communication strategies are also used to transmit messages about the characters' motivations and points of view.

The third section, *Gendered Expectations: Within the Home,* befits a drama which is centred on family homes and the emotional labour therein and the normative 'hatch, match, dispatch' domestic course of the female Ambridgian. At the time of writing, the volte force of Shula and her feelings towards estranged husband Alastair are a major storyline. Hannah Marije Altorf, in *'This Isn't About Curry, Alistair': Shula Hebden Lloyd and Iris Murdoch on Love,* uses Iris Murdoch's philosophies on love to give an articulation to Shula's position that the character has so far, failed to do. It has been commented on amongst the listenership that the birth rate in Ambridge is low. Carolynne Henshaw, in *Oh Baby!*

Unplanned Pregnancy and a Woman's Right to Choose, considers the actions of four Ambridge women when faced with an unexpected pregnancy and asks what we can extrapolate, if anything, from a comparison between Ambridge and UK statistical norms. Academic Archers co-founder/organiser, Nicola Headlam, continues her study (started in her chapter in Courage and Headlam, 2017) of who holds the power in Ambridge in *Women's Work?: Civil Society Networks for Social Stability or Social Change in Ambridge*, looking at Ambridgian women's identity and pressure politics, activism, voluntary and community work. Storylines and characters carry implicit and explicit messages around mental health, but how does this serve the women of Ambridge? This is the concern of Elizabeth Campion in *Strong or Silenced? The Under-Representation of Mental Health Problems in Ambridge's Women*, arguing that mental health issues in *The Archers* are unrepresentative, reduced to a plot device.

The fourth and final section, *Gendered Expectations: Beyond the Home*, turns our purview on women's lives in Ambridge to the wider world that lies past the front porch, into the village, and even as far as the Felpersham bypass can take us. Bill Pitt, in *Does* The Archers *Reflect Contemporary Values on Gender, and Sexuality?*, suggests that in order to reflect the wider society there could be more lesbian and trans characters portrayed in the programme, placing it in gender discourse and the gender politics movement from the 1960s to the present day. The careers, or lack thereof, of Ambridge women, is brought into a STEM spotlight by Jane Turner and Clare Warren in *Ambridge: Keeping the Pipeline of UK Female Scientists Flowing*: will the girls in Ambridge go on to choose science subjects, what determines who will go on to a career in engineering, can the current and future women of Ambridge flip the gender imbalance in non-arts learning and professions? From the science lab to the sports field, Katharine

Hoskyn, in *I Am Woman Hear Me Roar – And Now Watch Me Play Cricket*, considers the empowerment of Ambridge women (and correlating misogyny-busting) through their joining of the cricket team and puts this in a comparative context of cricket and sports in Britain. In *Sow's Ears and Silk Purses: Upcycling and* The Archers, Madeleine Lefebvre turns our attention to the entrepreneurial spirit found in the women of Ambridge and where and how this is located and extends the metaphor to spotlight the pressures felt by some to present a normative feminine form through their life stages and how this is internalised and acted upon.

REFERENCES

BBC Radio 4(a). (2015, March 15). How The Archers sounds to people who do not listen to The Archers. *John Finnemore's Souvenir Programme*. Retrieved from https://www.bbc.co.uk/programmes/p02mlwdp. Accessed on 26 August 2018.

https://chicagounbound.uchicago.edu/cgi/viewcontent.cgi?referer=http://www.law.columbia.edu/pt-br/news/2017/06/kimberle-crenshaw-intersectionality&httpsredir=1&article=1052&context=uclf.

Dictionary.com. *Intersectional*. Retrieved from https://www.dictionary.com/browse/intersectional. Accessed on 26 August 2018.

SECTION ONE – INSIDE AMBRIDGE

1

IN CONVERSATION WITH ALISON HINDELL

Nicola Headlam and Cara Courage

We were fortunate to be able to speak with Alison Hindell, *The Archers* acting editor from October 2017 to July 2018. Hindell is currently BBC Radio 4's commissioning editor for Drama and Fiction, having been its head of Audio Drama for over a decade. In this time, Hindell presided over *The Archers* in general, and specifically, twice, and most recently drafted in to cover the 'everything but Helen and Rob' aspects of the programme as editor Sean O'Connor faded out of Borsetshire and into London's East End (at the time of writing, he was *EastEnders*' editor). This tenure lasted until a job swap with *The Archers*' current editor, Jeremy Howe. We talked to Hindell about her time with *The Archers*, the work behind the scenes that impact the women of Ambridge and what she thinks of the women (and men) of Ambridge.

Hindell 'has always been a feminist', but not always a listener of *The Archers*. Graduating from Somerville women's college at Oxford, her career has taken her from the Royal Shakespeare Company to the BBC, but she confesses that she 'was brought up with a mother allergic to *The Archers*, "she [her mother] had a violent reaction to her mother's love of the programme, having been exposed to it every day"'. Hindell's 'career' as a serious listener began when on maternity leave, hooked in by the Brian Aldridge and Siobhan Donovan affair storyline. Hindell now integrates listening to *The Archers* into family life – 'It is on at the perfect time' – and isn't so convinced that listening on catch up is as easy as all that – 'It requires planning, making a specific time to check back in and isn't as casual'. 'Casualness' is not a word often associated with *The Archers* fandom. So many of us are so passionately invested in the characters that we never miss an episode, listening at 7 p.m., the 2 p.m. next-day repeat and then the Sunday Omnibus, and take to social media throughout the week to voice our differing perspectives.

Hindell's tenure with *The Archers* was longer than that of former editor, Huw Kennair-Jones; she is a contemporary at the BBC of the long-serving Vanessa Whitburn (editor, 1991–2013); and is at least the third woman (Liz Rigby and Vanessa Whitburn preceding her) to have been at the helm of the programme. Hindell was well aware of Whitburn's reputation for meticulousness and the strong grip she had on the whole world of Ambridge and she describes Whitburn as a 'strong woman and effective leader' in her stewardship of *The Archers*. But again, a confession, to some blind spots in her Ambridgology: 'I don't know enough about the detail of pre-Vanessa *The Archers* world. I have read the books on the history of *The Archers*, but there isn't much analysis of the scripts themselves, more commentaries and novelisation'. It was a similar search for a more detailed and critical look at *The Archers* that precipitated the formation of Academic Archers.

Hindell was able to open the door to the production room and answered a lot of the long-standing questions we as listeners have of the production and scriptwriting teams. There has been a lot of listener chatter about how the unforeseeable chopping and changing of editors has impacted Ambridge. Whilst she believes that her predecessors loved and treated *The Archers* with care, Hindell is firm that no one is bigger than the programme itself, viewing the role of editor as a custodial, curatorial one; 'Every editor', she says, 'should feel like a caretaker'. Anyone worried though that changing in editorship belies a lack of engagement, consistency or veracity with the Ambridge canon can rest assured that 'We aren't making it for non-regular listeners'. Yes, then, those in-jokes are written knowingly, and one is expected to research the long story arcs as they won't be presented via exposition.

However, there are long-term fans who have viewed the turbulence of storylines from 2013 to the present as stretching their credulity as listeners, and there have been howls of derisions at the various reversals in character and their behaviours. Is *The Archers* we are listening to now still suffering the wake of the Helen Archer and Rob Titchener storyline? This, Hindell admits, was an issue for a small team who were so totally absorbed by coercive control storyline, 'Because we were all on Rob and Helen, there wasn't a huge amount in the story cupboard'. Even 'the grid', a calendar chart mapping out fixed points for the storyline year, had fallen into disuse. Even so, given the sheer amount of time devoted to Helen and Rob, there has been a lot of storyline driven by the other characters packed into the subsequent years, but at what cost?

Hindell concedes that plot devices such as those around the Aldridge and Archer inheritances, particularly the manoeuvrings of Peggy Woolley regarding her children and grandchildren, had been due to the preferences of the different editors rather than any particular capriciousness on behalf of the character. Hindell comments, 'Had we known that I would be taking the helm for ten months in my second stint I would have been more proactive about various things, both in terms of management and of storyline'. Specifically, 'I didn't want to introduce another massive story while we were managing the fairly unforeseen mind-bending complexity of the chemicals in the Am storyline which has turned out more complex than we had expected'. Hindell continues, 'We set out to cause Brian major financial problems, but quickly realised that a landowner of this type would be protected against most normal eventualities so we needed to ratchet up the problem'. The tribulations and mooted 'Fall of The House of Aldridge' have contributed to Tweetalong grumbles about the 'Ambi-noir' nature of the recent storylines. This Hindell rejects out of hand, 'One of the challenges is that people think it is cosy but it [The Archers] has never been cosy it has always had powerful drama and storytelling at its heart'. Citing Jennifer Aldridge's illegitimate child, Greg Turner's suicide and Kathy Perk's rape as incredibly hard-hitting storylines from the supposedly 'twee' idealised past. Or indeed present: the jury scene for Helen's acquittal was designed to highlight social divisions in the UK in the post-Brexit referendum era, one of the final editorial acts of Sean O'Connor. However, she does chuckle at the notion of really turning up the jeopardy for the more established families in the village: 'One of Huw Kennair-Jones's first acts was to set up the Brookfield cow issue, which as a story was originally meant to be bigger than it was, and set up a feuding dynamic between the generations at Brookfield and their neighbouring farms'.

It is thrilling for us listeners to hear about the intentions behind the stories, but what of our plot predictions? When we suggest that people have seen the 'will-they-won't-they' of the Aldridges leaving Home Farm as a Brexit allegory, Hindell laughs, denying that it has entered the heads of the team. Still laughing, she says that there is 'a good PhD to be written on some of the political subtexts interpreted by listeners'. Hindell is far too diplomatic to suggest that the wild theorising by and plot predictions from listeners may be a little far-fetched, but is kind enough to agree with the Headlam Hypothesis (Headlam, in Courage and Headlam, 2017) that the wider village network is fascinating, and that both the Brookfield and Bridge Farm Archers are not families one would relish joining.

Much ire is voiced by us listeners around the lack of realism in Ambridge when it comes to both the farming business as well as the everyday machinations of community life: 'Village planning processes are often truncated' for dramatic effect and despite village events being 'realistic-ish', it would be dire if there were not dramatic licence applied to some of the more mundane aspects of village matters. The panto, for example: 'We have been known to forget to set up the necessary planning processes far enough out'. This may be in our favour though – us listeners are saved the year-round planning meetings that a village panto has, and this truncated version is still too long for many. At the 2018 Academic Archers conference, there was a brisk debate about whether mental health problems are under-represented in Ambridge or whether it helps to attach diagnoses and labels to people (Chapters 2 and 10), and with depression[1] as prevalent as affecting one in four in the population you might expect to hear more sufferers in *The Archers*. Here Hindell is circumspect: characters aren't labelled as having ADHD, or being depressive or menopausal per se, 'but there is a lot of emotional range on display'.

One cannot talk about *The Archers* without mention of the Archer family and its main clans, and Hindell talked at length

---

[1] At the time of writing, and prior to the beginning 2019 Elizabeth Pargetter storyline.

about the embedded issues at Bridge Farm, particularly how far the trajectory of the whole family was affected by the death of John Archer. In a sense it is through this grief that Helen Archer's vulnerabilities, so ruthlessly highlighted by Rob Titchener, developed, and the ongoing lack of certainty and direction expressed in that family is very much linked with their loss. Are the Bridge Farm Archers suffering a collective long-range nervous breakdown? 'I think these days people use the term PTSD too lightly' says Hindell, 'but there is something about the trauma of grief and loss' being played out over decades that *The Archers* can explore, 'What is of incredible benefit about *The Archers* is the "real-time" and "forever" nature of the programme'.

With the Helen and Rob story, Hindell is proud of the focus and attention that was brought to bear on the storyline: 'A vocal minority hated it, but I think the bigger ethical and cultural element outweighs it'. Hindell though is reflective of how far they moved the story forward once Helen had stabbed Rob: 'My view was that after Helen was arrested we spent too much airtime focussing on her being incapable of speaking and Pat blaming herself'. The role of Pat Archer in the Helen and Rob storyline was something that the writers took incredibly seriously, 'Pat as a mother and Helen as a daughter' and the spell the abuser places on and beyond the immediate family. Quite so: Rob gaslighted the whole listenership. However, 'Pat's brand of feminism was not what we were examining per se'. It was partly in response to the idea that Pat was too easily hoodwinked that 'we went on with the Olwyn story' to probe Pat's own sense of her ethics: 'She [Pat] is a very wealthy and financially secure woman now. We wanted Olwyn to remind her that life can go in different directions' Pressed on whether Pat's arc from obdurate second-wave feminist activist has been intentional: Hindell ponders, 'I don't know if I entirely believe in her feminism.

You could say that it is my fault as we haven't made it believable'.

There is also a quite bewildering array of practicalities in play: 'We can't make Emma [Grundy] an MP without precisely defining the constituency [and] we couldn't choose a political party for her without losing our even-handedness'. Similarly, she continues, 'We can't say which Oxford college Phoebe [Aldridge] has gone to'. When it comes to the working week, 'There is the fact that nothing ever happens on Saturdays. This might seem like a small thing but it drastically reduces our ability to use characters who work outside Ambridge'. Commuting to work, even into Felpersham would rapidly turn a speaking character into a silent one. There is the production working week too: 'Storylines can be hugely constrained by availability of the cast'. Famously there are only 39 booking slots for actors every week, which includes repeat uses. Thus, 'If Brian appears every day in a week, that is six of your slots gone'.

Hindell's concerns about the role and status of women in the world extended into her tenure as editor, but she is surprised to hear that according to our researchers (Chapter 5) that *The Archers* fails the Bechdel–Wallace test more often than it passes. Though for every criticism of unconscious pro-female bias seeping through, there are comments about the lack of female self-determination in the village. There has been much grumbling about the fate of career or childfree women in Ambridge, in that they largely have to leave the village in order to have a successful life (Debbie Aldridge and Brenda Tucker, for example) or that the professional purview of the women that remain is limited: 'Why don't women in Ambridge aspire to careers other than in farming or retail' asked one of the Academic Archers Fellows on Facebook. Hindell counters, 'I don't accept that. Hannah [Riley], Ruth [Archer], Pip [Archer], Jolene [Archer], and Pat and Helen all run big things with lots of responsibility'. Another common listener complaint has been that women rarely have a straightforward pregnancy, one that was wanted and planned and with an easy delivery. Hindell laughs, 'I agree with this one. I would certainly be interested in reading a paper about how contraceptives don't seem to work in Ambridge' as everyone keeps on getting pregnant from one-night stands or casual hook-ups. And yes, she admits to 'raising her eyebrows at Pip being on a quad bike ride so soon after a caesarean section'.

Hindell confesses having a soft spot for Lynda and Lily as well as for Emma's efforts on behalf of her family, and there is a theme (at the time of writing) in *The Archers* concerning the roles of women after their children leave home, with empty-nest baby boomers wondering what the next chapter holds. This can be seen clearly with Pat (though the Archer children seem incapable of leaving the nest) but also with Shula, whose divorce is the first aired in *The Archers*. In one sense it is simple says Hindell, 'Shula doesn't love Alistair anymore' but it is part of the phenomenon of older women initiating divorces in long-term marriages. The storyline is to ask the question 'Is there more to life?' When it comes to having a regular, consistently featured lesbian character, 'Of course' a lesbian character could stay in Ambridge. And here was the only trace of a spoiler. Having explained that the big question for Shula is 'whether there is something else out there for her', Hindell says that this will (probably) unfold happily for her but that the answer might not be a man...

Our Academic Archers Fellows wanted to know where the feminist activism was in Ambridge now, and were the Button Sisters it? 'They appear to be...As they were responsible for graffiti on Rob Titchener's car I imagine that they will be active in some of the call-out culture associated with the #metoo and #timesup movements. I have them marked out as demanding the stocking of Mooncups in the village shop!'

What of the men in Ambridge? Hindell is aware of the criticism levelled at the programme that the women of Ambridge are shown as more capable and balanced than their menfolk. It does worry her that 'the [Ambridge] men are "weak, feckless, irresponsible or even criminal"': 'Look at Freddie!...by making him a semi-aristo drug user, are we just creating another useless man?' It is, she concedes, 'hard to write good men in continuing drama'.

Further, there are those of us who have begun to wonder whether the demands of short-term dramatic effect add up over the years into some fairly dysfunctional inter-gendered relationships. 'Nobody knows where they stand even with the "good" dads' (read David Archer and Brian.) Moreover, one Academic Archer Fellow wanted to know, 'Why is pampering the answer to every female problem?'; 'Because male script writers think that solves everything'.

As we learn more about the dynamics of the production of *The Archers*, it becomes increasingly clear that it is a huge puzzle, and managing the equilibrium of this is something Hindell returns to repeatedly: 'Balance is key. I try hard not to let anything pull too much focus for too long'. One can see that Hindell moved between the lives of the numerous Ambridge residents, the village calendar, the arcs of the main families, comic relief and topical inserts with great facility: 'Yes, it is a complex puzzle and that is the challenge that makes it so fascinating and long-lived'. And let's be honest, whilst Harrison trying to form a cricket team, or Helen seeking out a new milk supplier, may not be edge-of-the-seat, cliffhanger stuff, *The Archers* does deliver on drama: 'One of the reasons that people like soap opera' Hindell says 'is that you get the juicy bits in your friends' lives and not the boring bits'.

REFERENCES

Headlam, N. (2017). Kinship networks in Ambridge In
    C. Courage & N. Headlam (Eds.), *Custard, culverts and
    cake: Academics on life in The Archers* (pp. 191–209).
    Bingley: Emerald Publishing.

2

'I'M NOT ONE TO GOSSIP': ROOTS, RUMOUR AND MENTAL WELL-BEING IN AMBRIDGE

Charlotte Connor, aka Charlotte Martin, and
Susan Carter, actor, in BBC Radio 4's *The Archers*

ABSTRACT

The introduction of female writers to The Archers *in 1975 brought a new perspective to the programme, revitalising its profile and cementing its place in the British psyche. This 'feminisation' of the programme was an important turning point for the women of Ambridge with increasing focus on issues important to them. This chapter argues that until this time storylines had tended to position women in the background of farming life, their identities shaped solely in terms of their relationships with the men of the village, as homemakers, carers and love-interests. The new band of female writers meant that the women of Ambridge were able to emerge as fully-rounded characters in their own right, as professionals, farmers, business women and matriarchs, at the forefront of village life. It goes on to discuss the character and function of Susan Carter, from the writer's perspective of both a research psychologist and the actor who plays Susan. It is argued that Susan utilises gossip not only as a tool with which to create interpersonal alliances and cement friendships but also to enhance her damaged self-worth and increase her status and power as a fount of all Ambridge knowledge.*

INTRODUCTION

The Archers first aired on BBC Radio 4 on 1 January 1950, following the success of a week-long pilot. The primary aim of the programme at this time was to disseminate educational information to farmers, interspersing this knowledge with tales of 'everyday folk' in a rural community. The programme quickly became a hit, attracting millions of listeners and establishing itself as a much-loved British institution. Despite its popularity, however, during the 1970s, listening figures began to fall, leading the BBC Radio 4 Review Board to seriously question its future (Henry, 2007, p. 205). The introduction of female writers around this time, however (there had been no women on the writing team prior to 1975), brought a new perspective to the programme, revitalising its profile and cementing its place in the British psyche. This 'feminisation' of the programme was an important turning point, particularly for the women of Ambridge, with increasing focus on the issues important to them. Traditionally, storylines had tended to position women in the background of farming life; their identities shaped predominantly in terms of their relationships with the men of the village, as homemakers, carers and love-interests. The new band of female writers meant that the women of Ambridge were finally able to emerge as fully-rounded characters in their own right, as professionals, farmers, business women and matriarchs, positioned at the very forefront of village life.

In February 2018, I was honoured to present at the Academic Archers conference at The British Library in London. This was not only a fantastic chance to meet the listeners of the programme face to face but also a unique opportunity to discuss the programme from an academic perspective. The conference was a complete success, and the day was filled with lively and thought-provoking analysis of the programme. As part of the conference, I was asked to act as discussant for one of the sessions entitled 'Ambridgistas – Women of Ambridge'. Two papers in this session focussed specifically on the role of gossip in Ambridge and, of course, as part of this, the character of Susan Carter, the doyenne of tittle-tattle and rumour.

THE ORIGINS AND SOCIAL ROLE OF GOSSIP

Whilst gossip may simply be perceived as the sharing of salacious information for entertainment, it has been argued that the fundamental social role of gossip is to create intimacy and influence (Foster, 2004, pp. 78–99). The original meaning of the word was derived from Old English, a conflation of two words, *God* and *Sib*, which referred to a close family friend, one who was deemed suitable to be a godparent. Rysman (1977) writes, 'Just as the "d" in God's spell dropped to form the word "gospel" so "God sib" became "gossip."' Whilst the concept of gossip is primarily associated with women – 'Shall she live to betray this guilt of ours—A long-tongued babbling gossip?... Then let the ladies tattle what

they please' (Shakespeare, Titus Andronicus; Act 4 Scene 2) –
I would argue, that men too can, and do engage in gossip, it
is, after all, the method by which we all, male and female
alike, inform one another about the society in which we live,
protect ourselves from those who, we deem, are engaged in
some wrongdoing or immoral behaviour and gain influence
within our social group. Think of Brian Aldridge and Justin
Elliot whose board meetings must be full of gossip and
speculation about colleagues and competitors, with the primary aim of creating and maintaining high social status. Few
men of Ambridge, or indeed, women of Ambridge, however,
are typically described as 'gossips'. Whether the gender, or
perhaps social class of the gossip, determines the way in
which they are perceived is up for debate, but, fundamentally,
for such behaviour to be effective, it requires not only a
perpetrator but a listener too. Therefore, I would argue that
when we castigate the gossip we must also reflect on our own
position in that dyad.

WE NEED TO TALK ABOUT SUSAN

Whilst its origins may be in the dissemination of farming
information, *The Archers* could be argued to have evolved
into a social documentary, reflecting multiple aspects of the
human condition through exploration of interpersonal relationships and social groups, pertinent to us all whether we be
in town or country, and with, therefore, gossip, at its core. In
The Archers, as in all radio drama, gossip is utilised to guide
and place 'off-air' events for listeners, keeping them up to date
with goings-on, but it also enables listeners to become part of
the drama and, for *The Archers* listeners in particular, to
become part of the Ambridge social group. This allows them
to empathise with or judge certain characters, as they would

do in 'real-life' situations. But, despite its functionality, in 'real life', gossip and those who engage in it, is often regarded as malicious and associated with small-minded bigots. It is Susan who has had the unfortunate luck to be perceived in this way, regularly reviled for her apparent enjoyment of discussing and commenting on other people's lives. However, Louise Gillies (2017) from Kings College, London, in her Academic Archers conference session (and in Chapter 4), 'In praise of gossip – why tongue-wagging and the rumour mill are important in Ambridge', pointed out that Susan is '...not a gossip, but a key player in informing not only fellow villagers of the latest goings on in Ambridge, but also the listeners.' As such, Susan's gossip could be argued to be integral to *The Archers*. This is beautifully demonstrated by the increasing use of Twitter by *The Archers* listeners. Tweets about the programme are brimful of gossip and criticism and, it could be argued, this highlights how it is the listeners who are the most promiscuous gossips. The Sunday morning live Tweetalong in particular is a constant stream of tweets extrapolating the activities, motives and moralities of a host of the Ambridge residents. This display of gossip and 'auditory voyeurism' serves the function of bringing together likeminded listeners, excluding others and forming strong alliances between *The Archers* listeners.

The question arises, therefore, as to why it is Susan who has been singled out as the malicious gossiper and who has risen to become the character we love to hate. One answer may be that her behaviour is associated with her gender and her working-class status. A subsequent paper at the Academic Archers conference (and in Chapter 3), 'Neighbourhood watch: Gossip, power and the working-class matriarch in The Archers', from Claire Mortimer (2018), University of East Anglia, explored this notion, proposing that Susan's character is perhaps 'informed by the comic tradition of the unruly working-class matriarch... whose excessive talk reinforces the social divide that she longs to overcome'. This suggests that the perception of Susan's gossip may be underpinned by the legacy of a social tradition depicting the powerlessness of working-class women.

Having played Susan Carter for more years than I care to remember, I have had ample opportunities to reflect on her in terms of her working-class roots and social status as a woman of Ambridge. I have been particularly interested in the impact of her humble beginnings, how this has driven her desire for social status and fuelled her need to possess and share knowledge about the intimate details of other people's lives. I believe that, as a working-class woman, Susan regards herself as powerless – she has no real wealth and no 'career', hence, little obvious influence – and that she uses gossip as a way of readdressing this power imbalance. From this perspective, it would seem harsh to criticise her for being a gossip, she is after all only striving for what all human beings desire – respect and acceptance. For the men of Ambridge, this is typically achieved through their career, but for the women of Ambridge, particularly those of working-class status, it is perhaps more complex: respect, power and acceptance are, even in the twenty-first century, still more associated with social class, femininity, attractiveness, and gentility.

So, perhaps, unlike the other Ambridge residents who engage in gossip, it is only working-class Susan's gossip which is regarded as malicious and unattractive, her wanton appetite for personal information typically perceived as underhand and with cruel intent, a thirst which seems unable to be quenched. But, I maintain that her gossip is not malicious, and, indeed, no different to the gossip of the more affluent, genteel women, or men, of Ambridge. Susan is not immoral or vindictive but flawed and insecure. She utilises gossip not only to increase and create interpersonal alliances and cement friendships but also to enhance her damaged self-worth and increase her status, power and respect in the village.

How did I arrive at such conclusions? Around 10 years ago I graduated with a PhD in Psychology from the University of Birmingham and now work as an applied health researcher at the University of Warwick, focussing on youth mental health and early intervention. Working as a research psychologist has definitely broadened my consideration of Susan as a woman and to actively explore the range of possible influences which may have shaped her character and defined her self-identity.

Susan first appeared in the programme as a young girl from the chaotic and infamous Horrobin family. In a dysfunctional and high expressed emotion environment, in which privacy was impossible and criticism and over-involvement were part of daily life, she regularly witnessed her brothers engaging in dubious activities and getting into trouble with the law, alongside her parents struggling to make ends meet and provide for the Horrobin clan. Such an environment would have communicated important messages to Susan regarding her social position and worth. The development of positive self-identity is, in part, dependent on receiving affirmations from those around us, informing us of our worth and value as a person. Being a member of the Horrobin family, however, may not have engendered many positive feelings in Susan and would have had serious consequences for her self-worth and identity. Such humble beginnings are unlike those of many of the other women in the village, women like Shula Hebden Lloyd and Elizabeth Pargetter, for example, who have benefitted from the presence of strong social support networks and the comfort blanket of financial security, who would have grown up feeling valued with the privilege that all these imbue. Looking out from her bedroom window on The Green, Susan would have witnessed first-hand these young women of affluence, whose lives, in contrast to her own life in the

Horrobin household, a life filled with chaos and testosterone, would have appeared idyllic and unattainable, in much the same way that social media today can serve to diminish our self-worth through incessant self-comparison. These early experiences have meant that Susan's narrative has followed a very different trajectory to the other women in the village. Her storylines have featured, amongst other things, an unplanned pregnancy, financial difficulties and imprisonment, all of which have led to an obsessive desire to better herself and increase her social status. We can see, then, that this drive may well be rooted in her early life challenges as a young working-class girl who wanted nothing more than to be admired, to be respected and to become part of the Ambridge elite.

MENTAL HEALTH AND WELL-BEING IN AMBRIDGE

Given my mental health background, I was delighted to be able to discuss Ambridge mental health at the Academic Archers conference. I have briefly touched on how Susan's early upbringing may have impacted on her sense of self and emotional well-being and how her experiences have defined her, and the conference confirmed that listeners were fascinated by mental health and well-being in Ambridge. Which characters did I think were currently struggling with their mental health? Did I think that Shula was depressed? Was Rob Titchener suffering from narcissistic personality disorder? Would Henry Archer develop mental health issues as a result of his early experiences? On reflection, I can name several characters who, in my opinion, have, and continue to deal with mental health issues (but I am not one to gossip!). The discussion expanded further to focus on whether the programme represented mental health as realistically and empathically as it could. *The Archers* has, over the years, featured storylines

about depression (Mike Tucker), suicide (Greg Turner) and
eating disorders (Helen Archer), but it was clear from the
discussion that listeners felt that such issues had only been
explored fleetingly and not explored as in-depth as they could
have been. Questions arose as to how characters who have
experienced mental health problems deal with them on an
ongoing basis? What specific help had they received? What
medication had they taken? How was their mental health now?
This led me to consider where exactly characters experiencing
mental health problems would seek help in Ambridge? Many
individuals with mental health problems spend a long period of
time experiencing symptoms before seeking help. Symptoms
during the early stages of mental ill health are typically low
level and insidious and often not regarded as problematic or
requiring professional help. When help is sought, however, the
first port of call is usually a GP. GPs are becoming increasingly
skilled in identifying and referring individuals for mental health
problems, but, in the absence of Dr Richard Locke, Ambridge
residents would now have to travel further afield to seek help
and attend a practice where they may see a different GP or
locum each time they visit. For those experiencing mental
health problems this is a 'real-world' issue impacting on both
the engagement of patients and continuity of care. And what
about the waiting lists for mental health treatment? Seeking
help is the first step, but we are constantly reminded that in the
'real world', accessing mental health treatment and support is
often hampered by delays in service provision. I would be
interested to know how Borsetshire Mental Health Trust is
dealing with targets and mental health service delays, let alone
difficulties with patient engagement and the challenges of youth
mental health...

What is the definition of mental health? The World Health
Organisation (2018) defines it as a 'state of well-being in
which every individual realises his or her own potential, can

cope with the normal stresses of life, can work productively and fruitfully, and is able to make a contribution to her or his community'. Yet when most individuals talk about 'mental health', it is often misconstrued as meaning a 'mental illness'. We should constantly remind ourselves that, as human beings, we all have mental health and that it is as important and vital to our social and emotional functioning as our physical health. The significance of our mental health, however, is often only flagged up to us when crisis occurs, and it becomes a problem, impacting on our interpersonal relationships and our functioning in society. Developing and maintaining positive mental health is crucial for our general well-being, enabling resilience in the face of life challenges. The majority of characters in Ambridge regularly display positive mental health and resilience; even those who have faced dark and difficult times manage to find the emotional strength to carry on. Helen Archer, a prime example of resilience, who, despite having experienced an eating disorder, her partner's suicide and a dangerous and toxic relationship, has risen resilient and renewed to make another batch of Borsetshire Blue. Where do characters like this find their strength and resilience? What lessons could we learn from them? How best might we, as a radio drama, impart these lessons? So, whilst I do feel it is vital for the programme to represent and consider a wider range of mental health problems, it is important that equal representation should be given with regard to those characters who display resilience and maintain their positive mental health. As such, the programme could play a significant role in normalising and encouraging general discussion of mental health, helping promote the importance of resilience and positive emotional well-being, and, subsequently, highlighting the benefits of early help-seeking. This would see the programme return to its roots as a vehicle for disseminating important and useful information to the wider community.

THE AMBRIDGE SUPPORT NETWORK

One of the key dimensions of ensuring positive emotional well-being is the availability of supportive social networks. This, to me, is one of the strengths of *The Archers*, which consistently demonstrates the importance and necessity of social networks and community. Villagers experiencing all sorts of problems are always likely to find someone to talk to. The range of Ambridge personalities means that whilst some villagers may be more approachable than others (!), a friendly ear, the offer of help and support, a cup of tea and a slice of cake is often just a scene away. Such support can be vital for those attempting to seek help.

Of course, we must remind ourselves that *The Archers* may not have survived as long as it has if it had become a one-trick pony, focussing specifically on one issue to the detriment of others. Its success has been that it routinely taps into not only serious and topical subjects but also the mundane and day-to-day minutiae of people's lives. This is what we love about *The Archers*, its capacity to portray dramatic storylines but also to focus on the size of marrows at the Flower and Produce Show and the antics of Hilda Ogden the cat.

I adore radio and the challenges it presents for actors. Our only tool, our voices, stretched to impart high drama, emotion, pathos and comedy for the pleasure of the listener. What I have particularly loved about playing Susan Carter for all these years has been her positioning in the comedic tradition of Ambridge. It's been a privilege to have been the recipient of storylines which beautifully showcase the absurdity of the human condition. The scriptwriters really understand what it is that makes Susan tick, and the scripts I receive each month are typically full of humour and struggle and an absolute joy to lift from the page.

However, despite her absurdity, Susan is, in essence, a 'real' woman and not a caricature. She is a woman who has faced difficult beginnings, who struggles to provide for her family and who constantly strives to make her life, and the lives of those she loves, as full and rewarding as possible. As such, she represents working-class women worldwide, women who hold down more than one low-paid job, women who struggle with their self-identity, women who just want to become the best that they can be, in a world beset with prejudice, discrimination and powerlessness; I hope she will not be disheartened and that she will continue to pursue her hopes and dreams and, of course, dear listeners, to challenge and entertain you for many more years to come.

REFERENCES

Foster, E. K. (2004). Research on gossip: Taxonomy, methods, and future directions. *Review of General Psychology*, *8*, 78–99.

Gillies, L. (2017). In praise of gossip – why tongue-wagging and the rumour mill are important in Ambridge. *The Archers in fact and fiction: Academic analyses of life in rural Borsetshire* conference, 17 February 2018, British Library.

Henry, D. (2007). *Life on air: A history of radio four*. Oxford: Oxford University Press.

Mortimer, C. (2018). Neighbourhood watch: Gossip, power and the working-class matriarch in The Archers. *The Archers in fact and fiction: Academic analyses of life in rural Borsetshire* conference, 17 February 2018, British Library.

Rysman, A. (1977). How the 'gossip' became a woman. *Journal of Communication*, *27*(1), 176–180.

World Health Organisation. (2018). *Mental health strengthening our response*. Geneva: United Nations. Retrieved from http://www.who.int/news-room/fact-sheets/detail/mental-health-strengthening-our-response. Accessed on 20 September 2018.

SECTION TWO – WOMEN'S TALK: INFORMAL INFORMATION NETWORKS THAT SUSTAIN THE VILLAGE

3

NEIGHBOURHOOD WATCH: GOSSIP, POWER AND THE WORKING-CLASS MATRIARCH IN *THE ARCHERS*

Claire Mortimer

ABSTRACT

As the foremost gossip in Ambridge, Susan Carter can lay claim to being the most powerful character in The Archers. *Ridiculed for her social aspirations, Susan is bolstered by her proximity to the world of privilege through her son's marriage to Alice Aldridge and her husband's status as chairman of the parish council. Within the village, Susan is both feared and ridiculed, giving her an ambivalent status in the narrative, yet she is pivotal in her role at the heart of the 'information superhighway' of gossip within the community. Her role is tantamount to that of a Greek chorus, commenting on and judging the actions of her acquaintances, her position aided by her job as manager of the village shop, at the heart of village dealings. This chapter situates Susan within the tradition of gossips in British popular culture,*

*exploring discourses centring on middle-aged femininities
and working-class cultures. I will examine how Susan's
character is informed by the comic tradition of the unruly
working-class matriarch, who is both strong and
powerful, yet whose excessive talk reinforces the social
divide that she longs to overcome.*

INTRODUCTION

As the foremost gossip in Ambridge, Susan Carter can lay
claim to being the most powerful character in *The Archers*.
Ridiculed for her social aspirations, Susan is bolstered by her
proximity to the world of privilege through her son's marriage into the Aldridge family, her husband's (Neil Carter)
status as chairman of the parish council and more recently
his appointment to the post of manager of the Justin Elliot's
pig unit. Within the village, Susan is both feared and ridiculed, giving her an ambivalent status in the narrative, yet
she is pivotal in her role at the heart of the 'information
superhighway' of gossip within the community. Her role is
that of a Greek chorus, commenting on and judging the
actions of her acquaintances, her position facilitated by her
job as manager of the village shop, at the heart of village
dealings.

This chapter seeks to examine the characterisation of
Susan within the context of the enduring tradition of battleaxes in soap operas and more broadly across European
cultural history, considering how social class and discourses
regarding ageing femininities inform such characters. Susan's
character is informed by the comic tradition of the unruly
working-class matriarch, who is both strong and powerful,

yet whose excessive talk reinforces the social divide that she longs to overcome. Susan belongs to a tradition of gossips in British popular culture, who are typically middle-aged, working-class women, and seek to overcome their marginal social status.

A DIVISIVE CHARACTER

The soap opera battleaxe often elicits a strong response from the audience, engaging listeners in a love/hate relationship, as is certainly the case with Susan. One listener was clearly flummoxed by her, asking on the Facebook page for Academic Archers: '…has Susan always been so insensitive, overbearing and self-interested – or is she designed to bring out that feeling of indignation in listeners?' Fifty comments were posted as members debated the role of Susan in *The Archers*. There was certainly no restraint as listeners ripped into the character: 'I can't stand her so vile and insensitive especially to Neil', 'With a friend like Susan who needs enemies', 'I hear that they are bringing back the ducking stool just for her.' The strength of feeling that she inspires is evident in this comment posted on YouTube:

> God, I hate her character, Susan! Such a nosey, nosey, NOSEY cow!!! Not nasty as such, but so stupid and selfish, and with amazingly loose lips that she always ends up being nasty to virtually everyone, and a lot of the time behind people's backs (though not always! Occasionally straight to their faces but because she's so dumb and self-righteous, she doesn't at all notice that she's blatantly rude!)… She's definitely my character that I love to hate! *(BBC, 2011)*.

Nevertheless other listeners felt somewhat more warmth for her, as typified by the following comment: 'Susan is the cornerstone of Ambridge. We should all feel indebted towards her! And her loyalty to Neil and her family show that deep, deep, deep down, she's a good person. We'd all be lost without Susan!'

Susan divides and provokes listeners, being a character who guarantees a reaction which is not always favourable. She is pilloried on account of her ignorance, her spite and her ambition – more often than not because she is opinionated and does not necessarily keep her views to herself. Do social class, age and gender play a role in positioning us regarding her character? Specifically, do we laugh at her on account of her working-class identity, and her presumption to aspire to a middle-class lifestyle? Does her status as an outspoken middle-aged woman who refuses to be quiet make her more of a figure of fun and the object of disapproval?

WORKING-CLASS MATRIARCH

The character of Susan is informed by the tradition of the working-class matriarch; a powerful force who dominates the family and home, and whose sphere of influence is felt in the wider community. Susan cherishes her position in the community, happily married to pig farmer and chair of the village council, Neil, she is both mother and grandmother, and holds down two jobs: working in the dairy at Bridge Farm and managing the village shop. She has overcome humiliation and disaster, with the character making national headlines in 1993 when imprisoned for harbouring escaped felon, brother Clive Horrobin. Susan was not one to let this hold her back, and both she and Neil have worked hard to attain a comfortable position in the community. She is fiercely loyal to her family, hardworking, and driven in her quest for recognition and status.

As a matriarch from working-class roots, Susan is informed by a tradition evoked by Richard Hoggart (2009) in *The Uses of Literacy*, when recalling the powerful women of his childhood in working-class Leeds. Richard Hoggart (2009, p. 29) recalled how the mother held the working-class home together 'more than the father', reaching the apotheosis of her maternal powers 'in early-middle or middle age, when she has fully established herself as the mother of the family [for] [s]he is then the pivot of the home, as it is practically the whole of her world'. The domestic environment is where the matriarch prospers according to Hoggart, the endless struggles and adversity consolidating her importance at the heart of the family and the community, and rendering her 'content'. Moreover, despite physical deterioration and the stress of struggling to get by, the matriarch is a survivor. Susan is repeatedly humiliated, and even imprisoned, yet her family have managed to better themselves, and she has managed to rise above her difficult start in life.

Middle-aged, working-class and outspoken, Susan belongs to a broader tradition of comic 'types' in British popular culture, as featured in the bawdy postcards of Donald McGill, with depictions of large bossy women and their timid hen-pecked husbands (Mortimer, 2015, p. 72). The figuration of the middle-aged woman as harridan and battleaxe has been a perennial source of humour, as with a long tradition of various soap opera matriarchs which can be traced back to 'harridan in a hairnet' Ena Sharples, the 'gossip and prophet of doom' who presided over *Coronation Street* from its incarnation in 1960 to 1980 (Thurmin, 2002, p. 129). Beyond soap operas, similar types can be found in sitcoms, such as Ma Larkin, played by Peggy Mount in *The Larkins* (1958–1964), Nora Batty in *Last of the Summer Wine* (1973–2008) and

Hyacinth Bucket in *Keeping Up Appearances* (1990–1995).
This legion of battleaxes are predominantly working-class,
strong-willed and unstoppable matriarchs, beholden to
nobody and comic in their social aspirations.

This tradition of the working-class battleaxe recurs
throughout wider European cultural histories, in Britain and
beyond, as typified in the monstrous matriarch featured in
Pieter Bruegel's *Dulle Griet* (1562). The painting was inspired
by Flemish folklore, with Griet being 'a disparaging name for
any ill-tempered, scolding woman'. Griet is depicted leading
an army of peasant women to plunder Hell; her warrior status
is indicated as she is dressed in armour, sword in her hand,
mouth agape whilst clutching cooking utensils. Bruegel was
painting at the time of the Spanish occupation of the
Netherlands, the figure of Griet being a celebration of fearless
resistance against the odds. Yet she is equally a comic figure
with her mouth agape, taking on the creatures guarding Hell
to defend her household. Could Susan be the *Dulle Griet* of
Ambridge?

The battleaxe works as comic grotesque, yet allows a visibility for the middle-aged working-class woman which is
widely denied within a patriarchal society. She is a monstrous
figure on account of her failure to comply with the feminine
ideal, manifesting qualities which are traditionally associated
with masculinity, such as assertiveness and power. The feminist scholar Kathleen Rowe (1995, p. 105) makes the point
that the matriarch 'represent[s] a dreaded domesticity and
propriety', being a 'fearsome or silly symbol of repression'.
These characters are 'set up as the butt of laughter' and 'may
be old and stubbornly resistant or indifferent to male desire,
fat or scrawny, shrill and "unfeminine"'.

Social class is often a vital factor in the formation of the
harridan. Despite Susan's perennial efforts to bridge the social
divide, her working-class origins betray themselves time and

again. Susan comes from a humble working-class background, being one of the Horrobin dynasty. Charlotte Martin,
who plays the role of Susan, described her character's background as coming from one of the poorest families in
Ambridge, growing up in a council house 'with cars all over
the front garden' and a host of dodgy siblings (BBC, 2011;
and Chapter 2). Susan's values are shared with the original
Coronation Street matriarchs, described by Dorothy Hobson
(2002, p. 108) as being founded in the working-class values of
the 1950s, a belief 'that hard work and gaining and retaining
respectability were important qualities'. Susan's social climb-
ing has faced various setbacks, which are the source of much
humour at her expense. One example was the *Calendar Girls*
storyline, with Susan nervously agreeing to be Miss October,
only to find her modesty betrayed by revealing a little too
much. Susan's nervousness over her body reflects her struggle
to assert her claim to social status within the village. She has to
be constantly vigilant about her image and that of her family
to ensure that she can stake a claim to be part of the Ambridge
middle class. As listeners – belonging to the largely middle-
class core of the BBC Radio 4 audience – we relish the
moments that the star slips from the vital part of Miss
October, and when Susan's pretensions are undercut. Susan's
hysteria over the family photo shoot, putting Neil on a strict
diet and agonising over her dress, is ultimately rewarded by
the photographer failing to show up and granddaughter Keira
Grundy vomiting over Susan's buttercup yellow dress.

Susan tries to set herself apart, and above, the other
working-class matriarch Clarrie Grundy, yet together they
perform the role of a Greek chorus commenting on the
events of the village as they work side by side in the dairy
at Bridge Farm. They follow in a tradition which can be
traced to the triumvirate of Minnie Caldwell, Ena Sharples
and Martha Longhurst in *Coronation Street*, likened by

Hobson (2002, p. 86) to a Shakespearian comic trio 'who commentated on the action from the snug of the Rovers Return'. Susan and Clarrie perform a similar role, connected by family and their work, more often at loggerheads than not. Notably, Clarrie is constructed as the more sympathetic of the two, accepting her role in life, which is that of constant struggle, and as the victim of the shenanigans of the Grundy men. Whereas Neil is constructed as the victim of his nagging, aspirational and assertive wife, a henpecked, loving husband, prepared to put up with the indignities of being Justin's stooge in his new job so as to keep Susan happy. Indeed, it is clear in forums how listeners demonstrate pity for Neil, specifically because he is married to Susan.

The qualities that render Susan a harridan can be seen from a very different perspective, when we see how she utilises her assertiveness for gain. The kefir storyline highlighted this aspect to Susan's character when she realises that she could play Helen and Tom Archer off against each other to improve work conditions and pay for her and Clarrie. Initially inspired by her customary competitiveness to try and beat Clarrie and impress Tom with her kefir, the rivalry between the two evolves into a sisterhood, as Susan sees past Tom's 'divide and rule' approach to management, and successfully manipulates the situation, making Helen believe that the kefir work demanded by Tom was compromising cheese production.

GOSSIP AND POWER

Despite her best efforts, Susan's body, voice and behaviour all refuse the disciplinary discourse of middle-class femininity. Actor Charlotte Martin explained how the character started out as a 'Hardyesque country girl', evolving with the years to speak with a broad rural accent, her voice being rather whiney and insistently grating (BBC, 2011). Susan's voice befits her role as a gossip, nuanced to wheedle information out of others. Knowledge is power, of course, ensuring that Susan is fully aware of the doings of the community, enabling her to deploy that knowledge to help consolidate the status of her and her family.

Susan's use of gossip is typical of the behaviour traits and purpose of the matriarch in the soap opera, described by Hobson (2002, p. 94) as 'both the spine and the nerve ends' of the form, their function 'vital to the progression of gossiping', which works not only as a recognisable character trait but also as a way of ensuring audience knowledge of the plot. Historian Elizabeth Roberts (1995, p. 208), in her research into working-class women in the second half of the twentieth century, observed how gossip was an integral part of women's lives; 'it confirmed their feeling of belonging to a social group with a common history, common traditions and shared standards of behaviour. It helped those experiencing difficulties in their lives'. To a certain extent, Susan is shunned and feared by the other characters because of her superlative skills as a gossip, for as Roberts' research revealed: 'Gossip was also feared; it could ruin reputations'.

Susan is at the centre of the webs of intrigue within the community by being located in both the village shop and Bridge Farm where she has access to a wide section of the Ambridge population, enhanced by her status as an in-law of the Aldridges and as wife to the chairman of the parish council. This positioning of the character gives her the potential for involvement across different storylines, her day-to-day interactions spanning social classes and the key families of the community. She is able to 'weaponise' gossip to achieve her goals, although her comic status ensures that more often than not such manoeuvres backfire, and she is once again humiliated. Her use of gossip gives her power and status, but equally works to isolate her as she is inevitably avoided in dread of her capability to disseminate people's private details.

CONCLUSION

Susan represents a marginalised social group in terms of her gender, age and social class, yet she is given licence and visibility within the tradition of the working-class matriarch in the soap opera. She has been largely deployed for comic effect since the melodrama of her incarceration and as such is true to the spirit of the carnivalesque tradition wherein the marginalised groups, such as the middle-aged working-class woman, are allowed visibility, voice and power. Gossip becomes a tool for Susan to continue her ascent up the social ladder, yet the comedy of her character lies in her numerous failures to pass as middle class. Ultimately, the status quo is maintained and the marginalised remain at the periphery of the community, the object of ridicule.

REFERENCES

BBC. (2011, January 21). *Charlotte Martin discusses Susan Carter's background.* YouTube. Retrieved from https://www.youtube.com/watch?v=JcySkfCOHdI. Accessed on 28 October 2018.

Hobson, D. (2002). *Soap opera.* Cambridge: Polity Press.

Hoggart, R. (1957/2009). *The uses of literacy.* London: Penguin.

Mortimer, C. (2015). Angry old women: Peggy Mount and the performance of female aging in the British sitcom. *Critical Studies in Television, 10*(2), 71–86.

Roberts, E. (1995). *Women and families: An oral history, 1940–1970.* Oxford: Blackwell.

Rowe, K. (1995). *The unruly woman: Gender and genres of laughter.* Austin, TX: University of Texas Press.

Thomas, L. (2017). The Archers and its listeners in the twenty-first century: Drama, nostalgia and the rural everyday. In C. Courage, N. Headlam & P. Matthews (Eds.), *The Archers in fact and fiction: Academic analyses of life in rural Borsetshire.* Bern: Peter Lang.

Thurmin, J. (2002). Women at work: Popular drama on British television c1955-60. In J. Thurmin (Ed.), *Small screens, big ideas: Television in the 1950s.* London: I. B. Tauris.

4

IN PRAISE OF GOSSIP – WHY TONGUE-WAGGING AND THE RUMOUR MILL ARE IMPORTANT IN AMBRIDGE

Louise Gillies

ABSTRACT

Gossip is part of everyday life and can play an important role in society. It has been part of human communication since we started to talk and is common to communities around the world. Evidence of gossip adorned the walls of ancient tombs in Egypt, and advice against gossiping can be found in the words of King Solomon in the Old Testament, in the theses of Greek philosophers, and in proverbs from all cultures. Yet gossip continues to be all around us, and most of our conversation time involves some form of it. Despite this, those who initiate gossip are often derided for being gossip mongers, and not without good reason. At its worst, gossip can destroy reputations and businesses, be used as a form of bullying, and cause a great deal of distress. In this chapter, however, I focus on why and how gossip is used and the purpose it serves in village life. Ambridge resident Susan Carter is a renowned gossip with high, unsubtle output compared to other villagers. I look at Susan's gossiping at both a psycho-social level and in terms of benefits she may gain. I also discuss gossip at the village level from two perspectives. I explore the importance of gossip to village life based upon peer reviewed literature, and relate these findings to the comings and goings of the residents of Ambridge. I then also look at how gossip is needed to relay storylines to the listeners. Finally, social media has helped to bring together Archers fans who like nothing more than to spend hours gossiping about their favourite villagers and berating Susan for her tittle-tattle. Yet The Archers wouldn't exist without gossip, so maybe we should be grateful to Susan and carry on gossiping.

INTRODUCTION

According to John Hardy (2011), there are two universal truths in life: one truth is that gossip occurs in all societies, but is ostensibly always disapproved of.[1] Gossip has thrived since humans could communicate. We have beautifully

---

[1] For anyone interested in the other universal truth, it is that farting is funny in all societies. Studies show that Ambridge residents do not appear to fart; however, one cannot imagine this to be the case with Jazzer McCreary (and who would find it far funnier than those around him) and Peggy Archer, who would probably become even more po-faced than usual.

preserved evidence of gossip from ancient Egypt drawn in hieroglyph form upon the tomb wall of the pharaoh Hatshepsut. Yet gossip has always been regarded as a negative form of communication. The Bible is filled with moral codes advising against gossip, and Greek philosophers have poured scorn on gossip. Indeed, we are still told that gossip is rude, hurts people's feelings and can damage reputations. However, if you want someone to listen to you, one of the best ways of grabbing their attention is to share gossip; indeed, gossip has been likened to the building of social bonds between monkeys and apes performed through the process of grooming (Dunbar, 1998). Rakoff (in Graham, 2016) has described the pleasure of gossip as being akin to schadenfreude – your pain is turned into someone else's pleasure when your secrets are turned into gossip. Yet in small communities where people live in close proximity to each other, it is difficult to maintain privacy, and this means that every event is regarded as common property and thus endlessly commented upon – a situation which occurs with each trip to Ambridge.

Without gossip, we would not be able to have our 13 minutes of *The Archers* pleasure (or pain?) every evening (or whatever your preferred listening time is). Gossip is not only the driving force of *The Archers*, allowing us to follow the goings-on in Ambridge, but also the driving force of fan groups who revel and delight in gossiping about these goings-on. *Archers* fans were asked about the biggest gossips in Ambridge: Brian Aldridge, Jim Lloyd, Jazzer McCreary and Eddie Grundy headed up the male gossips, whilst no *Archers* listener will be surprised to find out that Susan 'I'm no gossip' Carter was voted as top gossip, with close competition from Lynda Snell and Peggy Archer.

This very brief introduction to gossip takes research about gossip and places it within the context of Ambridge and

The Archers, looking at how it can provide a sense of community and belonging, its role in cultural and societal learning, maintaining order and for entertainment purposes (arguably, why we listen in the first place).

WHAT IS GOSSIP?

Gossip is a 'general interest in the doings, virtues and vices of others' which are informally communicated between at least two people about an absent third party (Oxford English Dictionary; Foster, 2004). Gossip is therefore a form of communication that can be used to forward and protect an individual's interests. In its original Late Old English usage, gossip was *godsibb*, 'a person related to one in God', evolving in Middle English to 'a close friend with whom one gossips' (McAndrew, 2017). The change of gossip as a noun to that of a verb was already changing by Shakespeare's time when he used gossip as a verb just once, Solinus saying, 'With all my heart I'll gossip at this feast' (Shakespeare, 2005a), by which he means the exchange of stories among long-lost relatives (Graham, 2016). The use of feast in this context is figurative; however, many of our contemporary synonyms for gossip revolve around social contexts and refreshments: water cooler moment, spilling the beans, juicy gossip, sharing morsels of gossip are just a few. The broad definitions of gossip lead to a fairly neutral concept. The problem arises from the fact that there is no nuance or understanding of the complexities that lie behind what is being spoken about. Good communication is based on discussion and fact, but gossip and rumour are based on one-sided judgements which are spread over a period of time. It is this combination of a lack of nuance and judgement which gives rise to the more malicious forms of gossip in particular.

GENDER AND GOSSIP

In *Titus Andronicus*, Shakespeare (2005b) used the word gossip as a derogatory noun to describe womanly behaviour: 'Shall she live to betray this guilt of ours – a long-tongued babbling gossip?' (IV, ii, 1841–1842). Whilst Western society still ascribes gossip as being woman's talk, research into the role of gender and gossip remains mixed, although recent research supports a greater tendency for women to gossip about others when compared to men (Davis et al., 2017). Both women and men gossip, but they do so in different ways: men tend to gossip about achievement, whilst women veer towards gossip about social information (Davis et al., 2017). Women are more likely to be engaged in negative gossip (Leaperand & Holliday, 1995), but female listeners to gossip do not respond in a negative way (Eder & Enke, 1991). Younger women have been shown to gossip more than older women, particularly relating to sexual rivals (Massar, Buunk, & Rempt, 2012). Looking into cultural aspects of friendship though, male and female gossip follows the friendship patterns: women tend to focus on close, intimate friendships, and women's gossip tends to be concerned more with family members and close friends, whilst men tend to have larger social networks and their gossip tends to be broader in scope, particularly around sports and acquaintances. As we shall see, these patterns do not hold true within Ambridge society, although negative gossip is more the domain of the women and comedic gossip is the domain of the men.

COMMUNITY AND BELONGING

Gossip is a form of social communication that bonds people together and is the human equivalent of apes picking fleas off each other: both activities involve spending time with another, cementing and maintaining social connections and cultivating a sense of friendship and belonging. For Susan, gossip is a tool which is used to try to build acceptance and friendship. In gossip, people share information about themselves and others within their social communities. In this way, gossip can be used as a way to maintain social relationships through the bond between the two parties spending time together in conversation and sharing information of mutual interest. The person who owns the gossip also has a sense of power: they own something that the listener wants, and this creates an alliance between those who are engaged in the gossip at the expense and exclusion of the party being gossiped about.

In the case of Susan, we previously discussed her insecurities (Gillies & Burrows, 2017; Matthews, 2016). Gossip helps Susan to feel superior. She may feel temporarily better about herself when judging others (Levin & Arluke, 2013), and this can also distract from what she might perceive as her own shortcomings or boring life. Gossip seems to be the only way she can rouse people's interests as she does not seem able to generate interesting discussions based upon knowledge and ideas. She also likes the attention, and gossip is the one thing that guarantees one to be *at* the centre of attention without *being* the centre of attention. Interestingly, even though everyone knows that Susan is a gossip, this also gives an illusory perception of trust, albeit in a fragile form; she is still fed potential gossip on a daily basis. Those who don't participate in gossip can be seen as untrustworthy, and if one is not included in the gossip, you are removed from the social network and cast as an outsider. Whilst gossip on the whole appears to be negative, concern for someone may result in gossip which was started in good faith but then perpetuated. Gossip about Kirsty Miller's miscarriage in February 2017 is such a case in question. Kirsty's friends talked about her and the situation because they were upset and worried about her, particularly when Kirsty was struggling. There was no malicious intent behind this gossip.

CULTURAL LEARNING

Gossip plays a central part in cultural learning by helping people to discover the rules for how to live successfully within their society (Baumeister, Zhang, & Vohs, 2004). This form of gossip is particularly useful for incomers and new generations as it reveals how the society operates, thus aiding assimilation and socialisation. Anecdotes, in the form of narrative, are useful as a type of gossip in which to communicate such cultural and societal rules and are akin to observational learning – we learn from what we see others do. In other words, we can learn from other people's triumphs and tribulations without committing any faux pas ourselves. Instead, we learn useful lessons from the mistakes and misdeeds of people from outside of our social circle with no cost to ourselves. At first glance, this type of gossip might appear malicious and damaging to a person's reputation. In many cases, however, this is not the primary goal, and if the story is repeated to people who do not directly know the person in question, there is effectively little harm done. For example, when Anisha Jayakody initially visited Ambridge, Alistair Lloyd provided her with information (gossip) and anecdotes (gossip) about the village and its inhabitants. She cleverly used this to her advantage once she had moved into the village by abusing her knowledge of Susan's loose tongue. Gossip is socially most useful when it has relevance and also enables the community as a whole to function more effectively through the provision of information. Whilst it is impossible to be present at each primary exchange of information, individuals within a society rely upon receiving information indirectly (Foster, 2004).

KEEPING US SAFE

Through gossip, societies can self-monitor and deter anti-social behaviour. This has been the case for centuries and still continues to play a part in maintaining law and order in some rural village communities in developing countries today. Not only does gossip play a part in keeping people on the straight and narrow, but gossip can also be used to punish individuals when they have breached the rules. The power of public opinion can be great, and it has been recognised in anthropological studies that people are often virtuous for fear of what is said about them and the damaging effect of negative gossip upon their reputation. There are, however, exceptions to every rule: given Matt Crawford's past, who would sensibly invest their money in anything that has to do with him? The village bobby, PC Burns, was not always needed: gossip reaching parents has stopped youngsters in their tracks when they were caught indulging in graffiti or involved in racial abuse. More recently, Pip Archer's failure to contain her cows, and the series of untruths that followed, not only cost the Archers of Bridge Farm in financial terms but also damaged the reputation of the farm as well as Pip personally. Such was the impact of the fence fib that it even divided the family. In this way, gossip both highlighted the violation and punished the culprit.

Gossip also plays an important part in health and safety matters. *Archers* listeners know of the dangers of joyriding quad bikes, having unprotected sex with ex-partners and never to climb up onto a roof with David Archer. If we fail to recognise danger, it can have far-reaching consequences. It is better to learn from someone else's mistakes than hurt yourself. *The Archers* also played a powerful role in illustrating the sense and intent of the domestic abuse laws within the UK with the Helen Archer and Rob Titchener storyline. The topic of domestic abuse had long remained a taboo subject, even in terms of gossip. Through gossiping about the storyline, it became possible to talk more openly about domestic abuse and helped to save a number of listeners from abusive relationships.

SEX AND POWER

Sex and power go hand in hand, and at its basest, this is what good gossip is about – who is potentially sleeping with whom, who is actually sleeping with whom and how this can destabilise the local pecking order, power and influence (Headlam, 2017). Ambridge has had its share of affairs of the heart (and body), and many have been gossiped about. When Brian Aldridge spawned Ruairi, his love child, his wife Jennifer was worried about her reputation and standing within the village. Lilian Bellamy used veiled threats to reclaim the power that Eddie Grundy had after discovering her sexual relationship with Justin before it was popular knowledge; this ensured that the information didn't get back to Susan via Clarrie Grundy. The interest in sex-related gossip is thought to be an evolutionary hangover from prehistoric days when cavemen were roaming Borsetshire, when reproductive success depended on the ability to navigate social and political complexities of communal life, that is – who was sleeping with whom. Those who were in the know would have had considerable advantage.

Gossip can also be used as a mechanism to further a person's reputation and to enhance their success (McAndrew &

Milenkovic, 2002). A prime example of this was when Brian
attempted to start his own gossip regarding his nomination for
Borchester Businessman of the Year, a title which he was later
not actually awarded, and no one in the village latched onto.
McAndrew and Milenkovic (2002) have shown that good
news concerning high-status individuals tended to be ignored
by gossips whilst dishonest behaviour was most likely to be
used against those individuals: few people (Ambridge
residents and listeners alike) seem to feel sympathy for Brian
and Jenny losing their home following the groundwater
contamination issues from the dumping of drums of TCE
(Shakespeare, 2018).

NO GOSSIP, NO ARCHERS

Poor Susan is regularly vilified for the role she plays as the
gossip of Ambridge, as are some of the other women.
However, without the village gossip, we would be listening
to a completely different programme. When one visits the
village shop to buy your groceries, you come out with far
more than just the products in your basket, and there is good
reason for this. Gossip is used as a process of information
transmission. Former editor Sean O'Connor stated during an
interview that *The Archers* works in its 13-minute slots
because of the use of gossip. Gossip stops the stories from
being piecemeal and fractured; we cannot observe all events
as separate storylines, so we depend on the gossip to know
who did what to whom and why. It allows an episode to
contain few characters yet keep us informed on other goings-
on, and hopefully keeps things interesting. Let's not forget
either how important gossip is in regard to the silent characters – we only know about them because they are gossiped
about (Chapter 6).

Imagine if we didn't have gossip: storylines containing only small talk between villagers. If all Susan ever talked about was the weather, it would become very dull. As listeners, we want pastoral, but we also hanker after something a bit juicier too. Another advantage of gossip in *The Archers* is that it purveys news secondhand, and in doing so provides a buffer for our emotions. The intensity of being flies on the wall of Helen and Rob's relationship proved emotionally draining for many listeners. As the abuse unfolded, we had first-hand experience of Helen's psychological ordeal. That story would not have been as effective if it had been picked up from gossip in the bird-hide or in The Bull, we needed to be there with them for it to be effective. However, we wouldn't want that kind of intensity all of the time.

For us, the fans, we spend a lot of time gossiping about *The Archers*, about the villagers, about the actors. We got outraged when Tom Archer came back from growing sausages in Canada with a different voice. We went into meltdown when Pip became even more annoying than ever and started talking strangely and poor old Sean O'Connor came in for a weekly verbal kicking (Furness, 2015). Social media groups have sprung up where we can talk about storylines and people, real and imagined. Without gossip, these groups wouldn't exist.

CONCLUSION

There is not a single reader of this book who hasn't participated in gossip in some way: whether you started it, perpetuated it or just listened to it. We spend up to 64% of our talking time in gossip (Dunbar, Marriott, & Duncan, 1997) and are 'hardwired to be fascinated by gossip' (McAndrew, 2008). Not only is gossip an important part of our lives, but it plays a key role in our favourite radio show. Let us give thanks to Susan and hope she continues gossiping for many more years to come.

REFERENCES

Baumeister, R. F., Zhang, L., & Vohs, K. D. (2004). Gossip as cultural learning. *Review of General Psychology*, *8*(2), 111–121.

Davis, A. C., Dufort, C., Desrochers, J., Vaillancourt, T., & Arnocky, S. (2017). Gossip as an intrasexual competition strategy: Sex differences in gossip frequency, content, and attitudes. *Evolutionary Psychological Science*, *4*(2), 1–13.

Dunbar, R. (1998). *Grooming, gossip, and the evolution of language*. Cambridge, MA: Harvard University Press.

Dunbar, R. I., Marriott, A., & Duncan, N. D. (1997). Human conversational behavior. *Human Nature*, *8*(3), 231–246.

Eder, D., & Enke, J. L. (1991). The structure of gossip: Opportunities and constraints on collective expression among adolescents. *American Sociological Review*, *56*(4), 494–508.

Foster, E. K. (2004). Research on gossip: Taxonomy, methods, and future directions. *Review of General Psychology*, *8*(2), 78.

Furness, H. (2015, May 28). 11 things that The Archers listeners complain about. *The Telegraph*. Retrieved from https://www.telegraph.co.uk/culture/hay-festival/11633573/11-things-that-The-Archers-listeners-complain-about.html. Accessed on 28 October 2018.

Gillies, L., & Burrows, H. M. (2017). A case study in the use of genograms to assess family dysfunction and social class:

To the Manor Born versus Shameless In C. Courage & N. Headlam (Eds.), *Custard, culverts and cake: Academics on life in The Archers*. Bingley: Emerald Publishing.

Graham, E. (2016). *Gossip: A quick linguistic history*. [Blog] Oxford Dictionaries. Retrieved from https://blog. oxforddictionaries.com/2016/11/08/gossip/. Accessed on 28 October 2018.

Hardy, J. (2011). Read all about it: Why we have an appetite for gossip. *New Scientist*, *211*(2822), 22–23.

Headlam, N. (2017). Kinship networks and power. In C. Courage & N. Headlam (Eds.), *Custard, culverts and cake: Academics on life in The Archers*. Bingley: Emerald Publishing.

Leaperand, C. & Holliday, H. (1995). Gossip in same-gender and cross-gender friends' conversations. *Personal Relationships*, *2*(3), 237–246.

Levin, J. & Arluke, A. (2013). *Gossip: The inside scoop*. New York, NY: Springer.

Massar, K., Buunk, A. P., & Rempt, S. (2012). Age differences in women's tendency to gossip are mediated by their mate value. *Personality and Individual Differences*, *52*(1), 106–109.

Matthews, P. (2016). Lynda Snell, class warrior: Social class and community activism in rural Borsetshire. In C. Courage, N. Headlam & P. Matthews (Eds.), *The Archers in fact and fiction*. Bern: Peter Lang.

McAndrew, F. T. (2008). Can gossip be good? *Scientific American Mind*, *19*, 26–33.

McAndrew, F. T. (2017). How "the gossip" became a woman and how "gossip" became her weapon of choice. In *The Oxford handbook of women and competition*. Oxford: Oxford University Press.

McAndrew, F. T., & Milenkovic, M. A. (2002). Of tabloids and family secrets: The evolutionary psychology of gossip 1. *Journal of Applied Social Psychology, 32*(5), 1064–1082.

Shakespeare, W. (2005a). *Comedy of errors.*, edited by S. Wells. London: Penguin Classics. Act V Scene I, Line 408. Retrieved from http://www.opensourceshakespeare.org/views/plays/playmenu.php?WorkID=comedyerrors. Accessed on 28 October 2018.

Shakespeare, W. (2005b). *Titus Andronicus.*, edited by S. Massai. London: Penguin Classics. Act IV Scene II, Line 149. Retrieved from http://www.opensourceshakespeare.org/views/plays/playmenu.php?WorkID=titus. Accessed on 28 October 2018.

Shakespeare, P. (2018). *TCE pollution makes life tricky for The Archers.* Retrieved from https://groundandwater.co.uk/blog/tce-pollution-makes-life-tricky-archers. Accessed on 28 October 2018.

5

'ALMOST WITHOUT EXCEPTION THEY ARE SHOWN IN THEIR RELATION TO MEN': AMBRIDGE WOMEN AND THEIR CONVERSATIONS

Sarah Kate Merry

ABSTRACT

In a village where the (audible) population is fairly evenly split between men and women, where most women of working age are employed or run their own business, where women are even (gasp!) in the cricket team, surely they have better things to talk about than the men in their lives? How often do the women of Ambridge talk about things that aren't the men of Ambridge? And when they do, how long does the conversation last? The Bechdel–Wallace Test was created by Alison Bechdel in her webcomic Dykes to Watch Out For *(1985), in which a character says that she will only watch a film that has at least two women in it, who talk to each other, about something other than a man. It is sometimes used as a simplistic measure of the lack of representation (not only of women) in the media. This chapter reports on five months of eavesdropping in Ambridge, using the Bechdel–Wallace Test to investigate gender bias in the Borsetshire countryside. The data show that one-third of the episodes during this period passed the test, while another third did not contain any conversations between women at all. The results include how often individual women speak to other women, which pairs converse most frequently and the main topics of conversation during the analysis period.*

INTRODUCTION

All these relationships between women [...] are too simple. [...] They are now and then mothers and daughters. But almost without exception they are shown in their relation to men. [...] And how small a part of a woman's life is that *(Woolf, 1929)*.

It is difficult to ignore the relevance of Virginia Woolf's *A Room of One's Own* to both the Bechdel–Wallace Test and the representation of female relationships within Ambridge. Although Woolf may have exaggerated the situation with regard to the portrayal of women's friendships in literature, it is as true now as it was then that female characters in all forms of media are frequently shown without agency and within the context of male characters' story arcs. In Ambridge, a village where the population is fairly evenly split between men and women, most women of working age are in employment or running their own businesses. And yet, even in this microcosm of twenty-first-century rural life, it seems that women's narratives continue to be formed and influenced by the men in their lives. This chapter uses the Bechdel–Wallace Test as a basis for an analysis of the conversations between the women of Ambridge during five months (February–June) in 2018: how often they talk to each other, whether they talk about something other than the men of Ambridge and whose conversations we hear most often.

THE BECHDEL–WALLACE TEST

The Bechdel–Wallace Test (also known as the Bechdel Test and, incorrectly, as the Mo Movie Measure) was created by Alison Bechdel in 1985, in her comic *Dykes to Watch Out For* (cited in Bechdel, 2005). The idea came from her friend Liz Wallace (hence the increasing use of the double-barrelled version of the name), and Bechdel also credits Woolf's essay *A Room of One's Own*, quoted above (Bechdel, 2013). In the comic strip, entitled *The Rule*, a character explains that she only sees a film 'if it satisfies three basic requirements. **One**, it has to have at least two women in it, who, two, **talk** to each other about, three, something besides a **man**' [emphasis in original] (cited in Bechdel, 2005).

The Rule was never intended to be more than the subject of a briefly thought-provoking comic strip; however, since the comic appeared online in 2005, the concept has gained increasing acceptance as a way of evaluating gender inequality in film. It is frequently used as an objective and simple assessment of the feminist credentials of a film (or other piece of media) – or, more accurately, 'to determine if a film has a strong female presence' (Scheiner-Fisher & Russell, 2012, p. 222). However, despite its popularity, the Bechdel–Wallace

Test has a number of flaws. It does not make allowance for works in which having few or no women is contextual (e.g. *Saving Private Ryan*, *The Name of the Rose*), and many films that could be described as feminist or a 'woman's film', or that have a strong female character who has agency and is not reliant on a male character to progress or validate her story, do not pass (e.g. *Gravity*, *The Avengers*). The Bechdel–Wallace Test is, then, something of a blunt instrument in its original form. A number of refinements have been proposed to the original requirements quoted in *The Rule*: for example, that the women should be named, that the conversation should last for over a minute (Sarkeesian, 2012) or that the conversation should not be about marriage or babies (Stross, 2008). It has also been used as the inspiration for further 'media tests' or 'critique tests' (Media Test, n.d.) used to evaluate other potential examples of bias such as race, sexuality and disability.

METHODOLOGY

In the absence of a standardised, validated version of the Bechdel–Wallace Test, a set of criteria had to be established. For the purposes of this study, these have been designated the Archers/Bechdel–Wallace Test (ABW Test). The first step was to define a qualifying conversation within the context of the ABW Test. Each episode of *The Archers* consists of a number of scenes, during which we may hear the beginning of a conversation, or join it halfway through. In order to be included, a conversation had to last for the entire scene; it was not included if (1) a man was present, even if silent, (2) a man was initially present but left before the end of the scene or (3) a man joined the conversation before the end of the scene. However, if another woman joined the conversation it was included. The other criteria are as follows: two or more women must have a conversation that is not about a man (a brief mention of a man may be allowed if it is in passing and does not significantly alter the topic of conversation: for example, Pip and Ruth Archer mention that Josh Archer will be doing the milking later); the conversation must last for longer than 30 seconds (an *Archers* episode usually contains between 4 and 10 scenes) and children under the age of 14 years are not included in the definition of 'man'. Therefore George and Jake Grundy (both born 2005) and Henry Archer (born 2011) can be discussed without the scene failing, while Ben Archer and Rúairi Donovan (both born 2002) cannot.

Collecting the data necessitated listening carefully to every episode of *The Archers*. Each conversation that took place between two or more women was logged, including the speakers, the length of the conversation, the topics discussed and how the conversation ended. This information was recorded in an Excel spreadsheet and analysed by hand. The period covered by this chapter includes the initial fallout from the Home Farm contamination. Brian Aldridge's acknowledged responsibility for the contamination meant that any discussion about the 'Pond of Poison' was ultimately about him. However, I chose to include some of Kate Aldridge's conversations about the fate of Spiritual Home, as these tended to be more about her own feelings than about Brian himself.

CALCULATING CONVERSATIONS

During the five months from February to June 2018, there were a total of 128 episodes of *The Archers*. Within these episodes, 200 conversations occurred between two or more women. According to the criteria detailed above, 95 conversations passed on content, but 10 of them were shorter than 30 seconds. Therefore, 85 out of 200 conversations (42.5%) passed the ABW Test. Although the aim of this study was to examine *The Archers* as a whole over a specific period of time, it is also interesting to consider each episode as an individual piece of media. For an episode to pass, at least one scene must meet the ABW Test criteria (Fig. 5.1).

The figure below shows that one-third (43) of the 128 episodes that constitute this study passed the Test, while the remaining 85 episodes are split evenly (or as evenly as possible) between those containing a qualifying conversation that failed the Test and those in which there were no conversations between women at all. This percentage is significantly lower than those quoted in the majority of Bechdel–Wallace analyses of films: the Bechdel Test Movie List (2018) has a database containing 7,829 films, of which

Fig. 5.1. Applying the Archers/Bechdel–Wallace (ABW) Test to Individual Episodes.

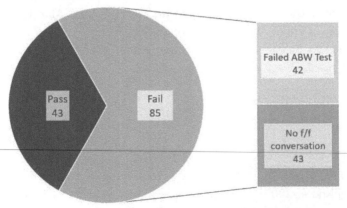

57.7% pass the test (though it is worth noting that the website does not use length of conversation as a criterion). 'Overall, there is a roughly stable tendency for the proportion of films that pass the test, at about 50–60% per year since the mid-90s' (Rughiniş, Rughiniş, & Humă, 2016).

The average length of time occupied by women's conversations in the episodes of *The Archers* that passed the Test is just under three and a half minutes. However, this figure is slightly skewed by a few episodes in which women and their conversations were the focus of the majority of scenes. The chart below illustrates this (Fig. 5.2).

The two episodes in which women's conversations constituted more than 80% of the total time were the episode in which Sheila Dillon visited Bridge Farm and Olwen failed to keep her opinions to herself, and an episode in which Fallon Rogers showed herself to be a dog whisperer and Elizabeth

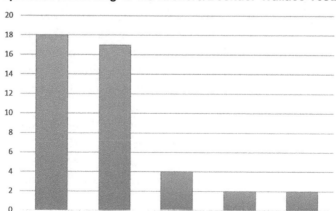

Fig. 5.2. Women's Conversations as Percentage of Episodes According to the Archers/Bechdel–Wallace Test.

Pargetter reminded Jill Archer that motherhood is about more than judgemental hooting. There have been a number of episodes recently, particularly during June 2018, in which every scene involved women's conversations, but they did not all meet the ABW Test criteria so this is not reflected above. For the overwhelming majority of the individual qualifying episodes (35 of 43), women's conversations about something other than a man constituted less than 40% of the total airtime.

LITTLE CHATTERBOXES ON THE (LAKEY) HILLSIDE

Conducting an objective analysis of something as familiar as *The Archers* can lead to surprising results: for example, Susan Carter's role as Ambridge's 'informal information network' (see Chapters 2 and 4) would suggest that she appears high up on the list of village chatterboxes, but in fact she is not even in the top seven.

The chart in Fig. 5.3 shows the 20 individuals who were heard most often during the analysis period, ordered by the number of qualifying conversations that they were involved in that passed the ABW Test. While Pat Archer is the most active in terms of passing the Test, Jennifer Aldridge had more conversations in total. Olwen is included in this chart since she had a noticeable impact on the statistics during her time in Ambridge and in fact she is the only woman whose conversations were exclusively *not* about men.

The table in Fig. 5.4 shows the data for dyadic communication within *The Archers*, where the pairs had three or more conversations during the five-month period. Once again, they are ordered by the number of conversations that passed the ABW Test.

As the most prolific communicator during February–June, it is no surprise that Pat tops this table with conversations

Fig. 5.3. Top 20 Individuals by Number of Conversations.

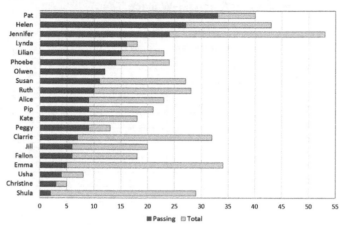

with her daughter Helen and with her friend Olwen. Pip and Ruth Archer had a lot to discuss during this period as Pip dealt with the realities of impending motherhood; so too did Jennifer and Phoebe Aldridge, as they dealt with Kate's reaction to the realities of the Home Farm contamination.

In a village with a high incidence of two or more generations of one family living in the same or neighbouring houses, it is not surprising that the majority of the dyadic conversations took place between women and their daughters, granddaughters, sisters and cousins. In some cases, these family relationships are the primary or only ones we see for those women. For example, apart from her interactions with Ruth and Helen Archer (her second cousin), Pip only spoke to Emma Grundy (once); Kate only spoke to family members, with the single exception of her conversation with Usha Franks during Usha's birthday therapy/torture/legal advice session at Spiritual Home.

Fig. 5.4. Dyadic Conversations, Ordered by Number Passing the Archers/Bechdel–Wallace Test.

Names	Total conversations	Conversations Passing the ABW Test	% Pass
Helen/Pat	18	14	78%
Olwen/Pat	9	9	100%
Pip/Ruth	16	8	50%
Jennifer/Phoebe	8	6	75%
Clarrie/Susan	9	5	56%
Kate/Usha	3	3	100%
Jennifer/Lilian	4	3	75%
Alice/Kate	5	2	40%
Helen/Susan	6	2	33%
Jennifer/Kate	8	2	25%
Jennifer/Pat	3	1	33%
Helen/Pip	4	1	25%
Jennifer/Peggy	4	1	25%
Emma/Fallon	6	1	17%
Jill/Shula	9	1	11%
Clarrie/Emma	11	0	0%
Elizabeth/Shula	4	0	0%
Beverley/Clarrie	3	0	0%
Emma/Jennifer	3	0	0%
Shula/Susan	3	0	0%

The conversations that did not happen between family members are perhaps more surprising than those that did: Emma only had one conversation with her mother Susan during a five-month period that included Nic Grundy's death and Emma's associated guilt and grief; the conversation was about the children's tea and Neil Carter's management pressures.

REASONS TO BE CHATFUL

The conversations that passed the ABW Test during February–June 2018 ranged from Alice Carter's drunken escapades to Christine Barford's dementia scare, via Lynda Snell's reading list and Ruth's 50th birthday party. In March, Pat reconnected with Olwen, a former activist friend, while volunteering at The Elms homeless shelter. As a result, the most common subjects of qualifying conversations during the analysis period were about Olwen – her brief stay at Bridge Farm, her life as a homeless person and her relationships with Pat and the rest of her family. Approximately half of those conversations were between Pat and Helen, the latter of whom was uncomfortable (to say the least) with Olwen staying in her family home. Another frequent topic of conversation between Pat and Helen was cheese and the uneven fortunes of the Bridge Farm cheese-making classes.

Ruth and Pip's conversations revolved around Pip's pregnancy and the resulting reduction in her farm work, as well as the ways in which motherhood would change her working life. The majority of Jennifer's conversations were with her granddaughter Phoebe about Phoebe's mother, Kate; during this period Kate's Spiritual Home business was negatively impacted by the Home Farm contamination and both Phoebe and Jennifer oscillated between supportiveness and frustration at her behaviour. On a lighter note, there were a number of conversations about dogs, as Lynda Snell searched for a replacement for Scruff by trying out a variety of breeds on short-term loan and, having selected one, entered into a dog-based rivalry with Lilian Bellamy.

OBEYING 'THE RULE'

As discussion and awareness of measures such as the Bechdel–Wallace Test has increased over the past decade, it is tempting to assume that there has been a corresponding rise in the representation of women in film and other media, but little seems to have changed, at least with regard to film. According to the Bechdel Test Movie List (2018), the number of films passing the Test has been gradually decreasing over the past five years, although as a collaborative crowdsourced database (Rughini et al., 2016) there is no guarantee of consistency across the ratings given. Since *The Archers* tends to focus on certain individuals or groups of people at a time, this analysis period was not long enough to give a truly accurate picture of the representation of women in Ambridge: Nic's death, the Home Farm contamination and Shula Hebden Lloyd's decision to end her marriage meant that there were a lot of conversations concerning Will Grundy, Brian Aldridge and Alistair Lloyd, respectively, and Olwen's arrival led to discussions which are unlikely to be repeated or followed up. A longer study of women's inter-actions in Ambridge may yield different results.

CONCLUSION

Eavesdropping on village conversations in Ambridge is amusing, informative and annoying in turn. Conducting this objective and relatively simplistic analysis of the women's share of those conversations has been an enlightening exercise and has confirmed the suspicions that led to the study. It is worth repeating that one-third of the 128 episodes examined for this chapter did not contain any conversations between women at all. The ABW Test data within this chapter indicate that, despite their qualities, their skills and their contributions to the agricultural and commercial life of rural Borsetshire, the women of Ambridge are not accurately rep-resented by the frequency and subject matter of their over-heard conversations.

REFERENCES

Bechdel, A. (2005, August 16). *The rule [blog post]*. Retrieved from http://dykestowatchoutfor.com/the-rule. Accessed on 27 October 2018.

Bechdel, A. (2013, November 8). *Testy [blog post]*. Retrieved from http://dykestowatchoutfor.com/testy. Accessed on 27 October 2018.

Bechdel Test Movie List. (2018). *[Website]*. Retrieved from https://bechdeltest.com/. Accessed on 27 October 2018.

Media Test. (n.d.). *Geek Feminism Wiki*. Retrieved from http://geekfeminism.wikia.com/wiki/Media_test. Accessed on 27 October 2018.

Rughiniş, C., Rughiniş, R., & Humă, B. (2016). Impromptu crowd science and the mystery of the Bechdel–Wallace test movement. In *CHI EA '16 Proceedings of the 2016 CHI conference extended abstracts on human factors in computing systems*, held 7–12 May in San Jose, CA. New York, NY, ACM (pp. 487–500).

Sarkeesian, A. (2012, February 15). *The Oscars and the Bechdel test [blog post]*. Retrieved from https://feminist-frequency.com/video/the-2012-oscars-and-the-bechdel-test/. Accessed on 27 October 2018.

Scheiner-Fisher, C., & Russell, W. B. (2012). Using historical films to promote gender equity in the history curriculum. *The Social Studies, 103*(6), 221–225.

Stross, C. (2008, July 28). *Bechdel's law [blog post]*. Retrieved from http://www.antipope.org/charlie/blog-static/2008/07/bechdels_law.html. Accessed on 27 October 2018.

Woolf, V. (1929). *A room of one's own*. London: Hogarth Press.

6

FOUCAULT, FREDA FRY AND THE POWER OF SILENT CHARACTERS ON THE RADIO

Rebecca Wood

ABSTRACT

The Archers *is a much-loved soap opera which relies entirely on audio outputs: on actors speaking and listeners listening. Despite this, many silent characters populate the drama. In fact, from Rosaline in Shakespeare's* Romeo and Juliet *to Godot in Beckett's* Waiting for Godot, *and not forgetting Tracey the barmaid in* Eastenders, *silent characters have long played a crucial role in dramatic productions, an influence all the more acutely felt if they are unseen as well as unheard. Therefore, using key examples of silent characters, and with reference to Freda Fry in particular, I discuss the expanding role and influence of the silent characters in* The Archers. *In addition, by invoking philosophies of language and silence, I will suggest they have an influence and potency in the storylines that speaking actors should envy, and that Freda Fry reigns supreme over all others.*

THE SPOKEN AND UNSPOKEN IN RADIO DRAMA

Perhaps the most obvious assertion we can make about *The Archers* is that it is a radio drama and so dependent upon speakers speaking and listeners listening. Moreover, we already know that music is used to enhance the plot in *The Archers* and to provide important, unspoken insights into the inner states of the characters (Baker & Jarman, in Courage and Headlam, 2017). Further, as well as music, a raft of non-verbal communication strategies is similarly employed in *The Archers* to convey important, unspoken messages about the characters' points of view, which they feel unable to express more explicitly. These include, for example, Lynda Snell's sniff and Brian Aldridges's har-rumphing, which regular listeners to the drama have come to expect in certain situations. Indeed, this non-verbal lexis has at times superseded its more conventional, spoken counterpart in both impact and popularity. Therefore, it's worth considering the extent to which silence, and silent characters in particular, might play their own role in what is essentially a sound medium, intended predominantly to convey speech.

For the purposes of this analysis, 'silent character' is used to denote a person who is named at least once in *The Archers*, but never actually speaks in the drama. So Kathy Perks, for example, who at the time of writing, has not spoken directly in *The Archers* for a considerable period of time, is not a silent character. But the late Mr Pullen, he of the dodgy waterworks fondly remembered by Joe Grundy outside the village hall loo, is a silent character because in his fictional lifetime, he didn't speak in a single episode. So let us now consider the influence of the silent characters in *The Archers* and, with the help of some philosophies of language, focus in particular on the role of one, leading silent character – Freda Fry – who arguably reigns supreme over all other silent characters, and even some with speaking parts.

THE USE AND FUNCTION OF SILENT CHARACTERS

On the surface of things, to have a silent role in a radio drama does not constitute the pinnacle of thespian achievement. Indeed, while some silent characters have existed for several decades, many others pop up to serve a short-term requirement of the plot, only to fade from view almost immediately. These include Joey the sous-chef, Roberta the sacked stable hand, Archie the silent boyfriend of Pip Archer and Evan Drexler the friend of Justin Elliot with the out of control Labradors. And not forgetting of course, Eddie Grundy's mate, the comically named Terry Two Phones. Therefore, many silent characters tend to be two-dimensional, existing only to support the development of those with speaking parts and details can be added at will, depending on the requirements of the plot. In other words, at first glance, silent characters appear to be unimportant in their own right, of low status, and dispensable.

What is striking, however, is the extent to which silent characters are used in the radio drama. Indeed, it is quite difficult to keep track of how many silent characters there are in *The Archers* due to the sheer frequency of their appearances in what is, after all, the world's longest-running radio soap. However, a snapshot survey based on a random sample of 10 episodes which I carried out between October and December 2017 revealed that on each of those days there was at least one silent character. The total number of silent characters across those 10 days was 22, which is an average of just over two per episode. In terms of the male to female ratio, there were 16 male characters but only six female,

although some of those male characters were the same people, i.e. they appeared more than once. While from such a
small sample, it's not possible to draw reliable conclusions
about the gender balance of the silent characters; it does seem
apparent that they are employed extensively in *The Archers*.
Furthermore, several silent characters have their own biog-
raphies on *The Archers*' website, of which there were 15, or
12.5% of all of the characters listed in July 2017. At that
point, there were nine male and six female silent characters
featured, one of whom was Noluthando Madikane, who
subsequently acquired a speaking part. So to be a silent
character does not necessarily mean never to acquire a more
corporeal presence in the drama: the unreal can become real,
and the insubstantial can acquire substance, power and
influence.

Moreover, regular listeners will be aware that it is unusual
for an episode of *The Archers* to not include at least one silent
character, and that on occasions, they threaten to both
outnumber and steal the limelight from those with speaking
parts. Indeed, names such as Becky Holden, Derek Fletcher,
Nathan and Neville Booth, Edgar Titcombe, Justin Bamford,
Richard and Sabrina Thwaite, Rosie Mabbott, Molly and
Tilly Button and many others not only evoke key moments in
the plot but distinct personality traits and seasonal highlights.
We know, for example, that Paul Blocker (also known as 'Fat
Paul') likes disco dancing, once stripped off to Black Lace's
'Agadoo' and recommended a loan shark to Eddie. The
annual Christmas panto also relies heavily on silent characters: in 2017, Barry Simmons and Nathan Booth argued over
which end of the horse they would be, for example. Therefore,
the silent characters help to populate and flesh out not only a
drama within a drama but create their own, off-stage spec-
tacles. Indeed, many of these silent figures have their own
character arcs as they grow up, form relationships, live their

lives and eventually die. Molly Button, for example, has evolved from a 'naughty' child to being a key member of the cricket team and a possible love interest for Freddie. And so it seems evident that without the silent characters, there would be no *Archers*, and that we can perhaps attribute its longevity at least in part to the existence of these shadowy, insubstantial figures who populate the drama.

Therefore, it's worth considering briefly how these silent characters might wield a subtle but undeniable power and influence in *The Archers*, even though, on the face of it, they are merely convenient devices brought in and mothballed when no longer needed. Let us turn therefore to some philosophies of language, power and silence before considering how Freda Fry, although never speaking a single word during the several decades of her existence, effectively, and in spirit at least, embodies these very ideas.

FREDA'S SILENT POWER

It has been argued that if we perceive language from a Foucauldian perspective, then it cannot be separated from notions of power and power relationships (Downing, 2008). Certain discourses and forms of language use, and the truths that they create, might be crystallised into institutions of authority, such as Damara Capital, Borchester Land, Berrow Farm or even the village shop and the parish council. Or they might centre on certain individuals who wield their power, particularly through the language they use. In this context, characters such as Justin, Brian, the Latin-speaking Jim Lloyd or, notoriously, Rob Titchener, spring to mind. In fact, for the Belgian philosopher and feminist Irigaray (1981), these predominantly masculine, governing discourses can be described as 'phallogocentric', where *logos*, the word, is used to oppress or marginalise others, and women in particular. Similarly, according to Liasidou (2012, p. 97), these forms of language use 'produce and sustain relations of power', and we see examples of this through board meetings, contracts issued or even, in the case of Susan Carter who rather brilliantly bucks this phallogocentric trend, through the power of gossip (and see Chapters 2 and 4). Therefore, it would seem that according to these ideas, silent characters are especially disempowered, picked up and dropped at will, entirely unimportant.

However, the ideas of Foucault and others have also been shown to support the notion that silence, and non-speaking, can be more powerful than verbal discourses themselves. Humphry (2014) has explored the notion of the 'pause' from a Foucauldian perspective. Humphry considers that according to Foucault's ideas, gaps in speech, silences and hesitations enable a 'different truth' (Humphry, 2014, p. 493) to be expressed about people considered to be dysfunctional and marginalised. Similarly, Acheson (2008), informed by the ideas of Merleau-Ponty, has challenged the idea of linguistic silences as something missing, an empty framework, a void simply waiting to be filled by speech. Acheson explains the high value which can be placed on silence in different cultures, where it can be both valued and interpreted differently. For her, silences can in fact be 'gestures', a form of communication which is more powerful than speech (Acheson, 2008, p. 552), and must be understood within the cultural, historical and intersubjective situations in which they are produced. And so, according to these ideas, silence is both powerful and empowering, and silent characters emerge as crucial in *The Archers*, acquiring a presence and a role in the drama more potent than some of those with speaking parts.

Let us now exemplify these ideas via the silent character Freda Fry, who continues to play a part in the drama despite the fact that she has never spoken a single word, and she is now in fact dead. Indeed, the actor Eric Allan who plays her widow, Bert Fry, said the following after her demise: '... she's only silent for the listener. She's never been silent for me. I've always had a strong impression of her as a real person. It's not a visual image, it's emotional – a very strong feeling of her presence' (Davies, 2015). Over the years, we have learnt a great deal about Freda, such as that she was a light sleeper, that she cooked an unrivalled hotpot at The Bull and her favourite film was *Guys and Dolls*. There is also the Freda Fry rose, and poetry written by Bert in her honour. Freda had regular successes at the Flower and Produce Show, and there is now a Freda Fry Memorial Award, first won in 2017 by another silent character, Cecil Jackson, in an episode which was completely dominated by silent characters (*The Archers*, 17 September 2017). Listeners will recall that when Cecil won, he celebrated by dancing, i.e. not speaking. Furthermore, in that same episode, there was also a reference to Cecil's daughter, showing how silent characters can spawn additional, secondary silent characters and even their own character networks. Moreover, it is Freda who is often the axis for these networks and plot developments.

In fact, characters with speaking parts can come and go, or appear very rarely in the drama, or even get dropped completely. But silent characters, like Freda, remain thoroughly ensconced in *The Archers*, with the scriptwriters having to continue to account for her existence, and perpetuate her influence, even beyond the imaginary grave. Moreover, perhaps the ultimate accolade was that when Freda died in the Ambridge flood, Banks-Smith (2015) wrote a newspaper column dedicated to her and even compared her with the Queen. Moreover, the presence of silent characters in *The Archers* also derives from a long-standing literary and dramatic tradition. There is Rosaline in Shakespeare's *Romeo and Juliet*, Godot in Beckett's *Waiting for Godot* and Tracy the barmaid in *Eastenders*, whose sacking caused national outrage. There are also musical equivalents such as John Cage's *Four Minutes and 33 Seconds of Silence*.

These examples prove not only that silent characters impact on the drama in ways we might not be aware of, but that their role is not to be underestimated. If Foucault showed us the intimate connections between language, meaning and power, his work also suggests that meaning is not only achieved through what is spoken, and that the physical act of speech can be superseded by other forms of communication, including silence. We see this so clearly in many silent characters in *The Archers*, but Freda Fry in particular. Not only this, but *The Archers*, in featuring so many silent characters, emerges as a radical drama, extending this literary tradition into brave new territories, that of the radio-listening medium, the ultimate taboo. What next? Perhaps an episode of *The Archers* consisting only of silent characters, punctuated by the mooing of cows, the baaing of sheep, an occasional sniff, and the gentle sound of the Freda Fry rose, blowing in the breeze.

REFERENCES

Acheson, K. (2008). Silence as gesture: Rethinking the nature of communicative silences. *Communication Theory*, *18*, 535–555.

Baker, E., & Jarman, F. (2017). Soundtrack to a stabbing: What Rob's choice of music over dinner tells us about why he ended up spilling the custard. In C. Courage & N. - Headlam (Eds.), *Custard, culverts and cake: Academics in life in The Archers*. Bingley: Emerald Publishing.

Banks-Smith, N. (2015, March 24). Nancy Banks-Smith on the Archers: After the flood. *The Guardian*. Retrieved from https://www.theguardian.com/tv-and-radio/2015/mar/24/a-month-in-ambridge-great-flood-freda-death. Accessed on 4 February 2018.

Davies, K. (2015, March 11). Freda Fry RIP. *The Archers* blog. Retrieved from http://www.bbc.co.uk/blogs/the-archers/entries/684cb733-8a22-4b35-92ba-e23200b201f3. Accessed 15 January 2018.

Downing, L. (2008). *The Cambridge introduction to Michel Foucault*. Cambridge: Cambridge University Press.

Humphry, N. (2014). Disrupting deficit: The power of "the pause" in resisting the dominance of deficit knowledges in education. *International Journal of Inclusive Education*, *18*(5), 484–499.

Irigaray, L. (1981). The sex which is not one. In E. Marks & I. de Courtivron (Eds.), *New French feminisms*. Brighton: The Harvester Press Limited.

Liasidou, A. (2012). *Inclusive education, politics and policy-making*. London: Continuum International Publishing Group.

SECTION THREE – GENDERED EXPECTATIONS: WITHIN THE HOME

7

'THIS ISN'T ABOUT CURRY, ALISTAIR': SHULA HEBDEN LLOYD AND IRIS MURDOCH ON LOVE

Hannah Marije Altorf

ABSTRACT

This paper reflects on the divorce between The Archer's *Shula and Alistair Hebden Lloyd. It considers in particular Shula's main reason for the separation ('I just don't love you anymore') and her inability to explain any further ('It's just how I feel'). It does so by bringing Shula in conversation with the British philosopher and novelist Iris Murdoch, who was an avid listener to* The Archers. *Love is for Murdoch a moral virtue, though she is also aware of its trappings. I shall use the recent scholarly debate on the love in Murdoch's work to help Shula reflect on her claim.*

> Should an unhappy marriage be continued for the children? ... The love which brings the right answer is an exercise of justice and realism and really looking. *(Murdoch, 2001)*

On 14 March 2018, after a sleepless night, Shula Hebden Lloyd realises that her marriage is over (BBC Radio 4b). She does not love Alistair, her husband, anymore. In subsequent weeks, the separation unfolds, featuring all the elements that may be so familiar to those who have experienced such breakups from close by. One party is relieved while the other is overcome by feelings of disbelief, shock and humiliation. People around them rally to help, to admonish or to take sides.

Some of the most difficult conversations that follow concern Shula's reason for the separation, as well as her inability to explain any further: 'It's just how I feel. I just don't love you anymore' (BBC Radio 4b). Not loving Alistair any longer is the main reason for declaring her marriage over. Shula keeps repeating it: to her brother Kenton Archer, to whom she runs after leaving the house, to her mother (Jill Archer) after church and to Alistair at the top of her voice at the exact moment when the scriptwriters, rather cruelly, stage their son Dan's return home. Shula's explanation is either taken at face value (by Kenton and by her sister Elizabeth Pargetter) or not believed (by Alistair and Dan) or denied any significance (by Jill). Shula rarely doubts the validity of her reason for leaving Alistair. Yet, she is not convincing when explaining it. Any further explanation is put either rather selfishly, ('What I need to be happy', BBC Radio 4c) or in terms of determinism. Both return in the rather clichéd language of her understanding brother and sister: 'You have to be true to your feelings', '…things just run their course' (BBC Radio 4b), 'Relationships just reach the end of the road' (BBC Radio 4e). It is this kind of language that Alistair objects to, comparing it to a 'car crash where no one is liable' (BBC Radio 4f).

This chapter intends to come to Shula's rescue by suggesting a moral vision and moral vocabulary to help understand and explain her situation. It does so by bringing Shula in conversation with the British philosopher and novelist Iris Murdoch. Murdoch was an avid listener of *The Archers* (Warnock, 2002, pp. 81–82) and she understood love as central to moral philosophy, even though she was also aware of its trappings. The comparison suggested itself when I was listening to the divorce unfold, while also researching recent scholarship on Murdoch and noticing the growing number of publications on Murdoch and love. I was moved by Shula's honest acknowledgement and annoyed by the patriarchal admonishment of her husband, her son and her mother. I was also frustrated with Shula, and perhaps even more the scriptwriters, for her being paralysed by guilt. This chapter is, then, more than an attempt to use the recent scholarly debate on love in Murdoch's work to help Shula reflect on her claim or to understand Murdoch by considering an example. It is also a defence of Shula and a plea to take a woman at her word. I shall argue that by taking love so seriously Shula has grasped a fundamental aspect of what it is to be human. We are principally motivated by love and our love needs to be directed well for us to become morally better. Before I proceed, I should add that this article was written in the early summer of 2018, while the storyline was unfolding. Since then, it may have developed in a direction which asks for further or different reflections.

To introduce Murdoch's ideas it is helpful to distinguish different philosophical positions in the responses of characters to Shula's announcement. The extent to which others believe Shula can be related to the philosophical position they take. Kenton, for instance, is a bit of a hedonist and thus for him a profound feeling of unhappiness is sufficient ground to do something about it. He accepts Shula's reason without much persuasion. Jill, in contrast, is much more sceptical and has difficulty believing Shula, ('We all go through phases like that!', BBC Radio 4h). Jill's response is her own mixture of traditional defence of marriage and principled reasoning. Indeed, Jill often resorts to principle. More than once she asks Shula: 'Do your wedding vows mean nothing to you?' (BBC Radio 4d, 4h), to which Shula has difficulty finding an answer. She first calls the question unfair and then mutters that they did when she said them. This, of course, fundamentally undermines the notion of a vow and perhaps not surprisingly Jill keeps brushing Shula's concerns away. Jill's partiality to principle, as well as its inaptitude, is reaffirmed even in their eventual reconciliation, as it is initiated by an abstract principle she learnt from her other daughter, Elizabeth: mothers support their children (BBC Radio 4a). Jill declares it with some pride and Shula is, not surprisingly, nonplussed. The real reconciliation has to wait for the moment when Jill asks in a quivering voice for a hug. Shula starts crying and the two women embrace.

The most irreconcilable difference is, not surprisingly, between Shula and Alistair. They are, as Shula puts it, on 'completely different wave lengths', ('This isn't about curry, Alistair', BBC Radio 4c). When Shula first tells Alistair that she does not love him anymore, she presents it as irretrievable fact: 'It's just how I feel. I just don't love you anymore'. Perhaps encouraged by the repetition of 'just' and the emphasis on feeling, Alistair does not judge the situation as beyond repair. After Shula flees the house, he shouts after her: 'We need to talk about this!' (BBC Radio 4b). Alistair claims reason and argument. From the very first day he calls the situation 'stupid', 'madness' and 'insane' and in the first few weeks after Shula's announcement – including immediately after she tells him that she does not love him anymore – he demands that they talk. At one point, he suggests that Shula and he get counselling, so that she may understand why she stopped loving him and then undo the decision. Alistair believes that insight in the causes may make her change her mind. However, when none of his suggestions appear to be welcome, reason goes out the window. He first reverts to magical thinking, where the universe, in the guise of his wife (Shula) and his partner in the veterinary practice (Anisha Jayakody), has turned against him, and next to gambling.

I would argue that to a certain extent Alistair represents the philosophical position that Murdoch describes in her seminal *The Sovereignty of Good* as 'ideally rational man'. Murdoch introduces this 'man' in 'The Idea of Perfection', as 'more or less explicitly lurking behind much that is written nowadays on the subject of moral philosophy and indeed also of politics' (Murdoch, 2001, pp. 6–7). This 'man' should know his intentions, he rationally considers all the options that are open to everyone to see and then chooses. Alistair resembles this man, for instance, when he keeps referring to Shula's 'decision' and suggests counselling, on the assumption that if Shula knows her intentions she may undo her initial decision and choose differently. He too finds it hard to accept that he did not see this coming or perhaps even that he may never be able to see the situation fully.

Understandable as his suggestions are from the perspective of a husband who, as he exclaims to Kenton, 'does not know what planet he is on' (BBC Radio 4b), they are rebuffed and lead nowhere. That fact may be one indication of their limitations. Another is his turn to magical thinking and gambling. As Murdoch puts it: 'I do not think people are necessarily or essentially "like that"' (Murdoch, 2001, p. 9). Murdoch formulates different objections to 'ideally rational man'. Most importantly, she objects to a moral philosophy that emphasises action and choice. In its stead, she seeks to develop a moral philosophy in which love plays a central role again, one which recognises the significance of a loving vision.

Love is a central concept for Murdoch's moral philosophy. As she claims in *The Sovereignty of Good* (Murdoch, 2001, p. 45; cp. p. 2): 'We need a moral philosophy in which the concept of love, so rarely mentioned now by philosophers, can once again be made central'. Given this explicit proposal, it is surprising that the notion only received limited attention in Murdoch scholarship until recently. This oversight may be partly explained by love's ambiguous nature. Love can be spiritual as well as possessive (about which more later). It should not surprise then that Murdoch, while proclaiming the significance of love, does not discuss it at great length and that the topic has long been marginal in the philosophical scholarship.

Love is, Murdoch writes in 'The Sublime and the Good' (1997, p. 215; cp. Merritt, 2017, p. 1845), 'the extremely difficult realisation that something other than oneself is real. Love…is the discovery of reality'. For Murdoch, looking with love is not seeing through rose-coloured glasses, but neither is really seeing something purely objective. To see lovingly is to see it for what it really is and to really see is to see lovingly. Here I return to the quotation at the beginning of this article (Murdoch, 2001, p. 89):

> Should a retarded child be kept at home or sent to an institution? Should an elderly relation who is a trouble-maker be cared for or asked to go away? Should an unhappy marriage be continued for the sake of the children? Should I leave my family in order to do political work? The love which brings the right answer is an exercise of justice and realism and really looking. … It is a task to come to see the world as it is.

The focus of the moral life, for Murdoch, is then not choice, but the 'endless' task of looking and loving (Murdoch, 2001, p. 23). Is this what Shula was doing during her sleepless night?

Given that Plato is the most important inspiration for Murdoch's understanding of love, the question rises what the 'something other than oneself' is: a particular other or the idea of the Good? Commentators, most notably Gregory Vlastos, have criticised Plato for subordinating the individual to the Good. The lover is not loved as himself, but in order for the lover to progress to the higher forms (Vlastos, 1973, cited in; Hopwood, 2018, p. 490). Whether this criticism is justified where Plato is concerned, I leave for another time. For now, it suffices to show that it does not apply to Murdoch. As Mark Hopwood argues, for Murdoch we love both the Good and individuals. For Murdoch, 'Good is the magnetic centre towards which love naturally moves', but she also provides examples in which love is directed towards individuals (2001, p. 100). As Hopwood (2018, p. 486) puts it 'in the form of a slogan: We love particular individuals in the light of the good, and we love the good through particular individuals'. For Murdoch one does not love the individual at the cost of the Good or the Good at the cost of the individual, though she also realises that there is often tension between the two.

Why, lastly, is it 'extremely difficult' to realise that the other is real? Murdoch argues that we have to overcome egoism and fantasy, and this is not easy. Her argument starts from what she confesses to be a rather 'depressing description' of human beings: 'human beings are naturally selfish...'. We are constantly consoling our hurt egos in fantasies and daydreams. We are not as free as we think (Murdoch, 2001, pp. 76–77). It is not easy to escape this predicament. Here love plays again a role. A way out of our selfish daydreams is by loving. Love itself can be the great motivator to undo our fantasies (as it is for Plato, Nussbaum, 2012, p. 139). Love can help us to start learning about reality again (Nussbaum, 2012, p. 136). Indeed, for Murdoch, falling in love may exactly do that: 'Falling in love is for many people their most intense experience, bringing with it a quasi-religious certainty, and most disturbing because it shifts the centre of the world from the outside to another place' (Murdoch, 1993, pp. 16–17; cp. Hopwood, 2018, pp. 489–490).

Is this what happened to Shula? As the story unfolds we learn that crucial insight was gained by her feeling briefly attracted to builder Philip Moss, as she confesses at one point to her cousin Lilian. As for the soul in Plato's *Phaedrus*, falling in love, even if only so briefly, helped her see what is missing and remember the love and the joy she once had (Plato, *Phaedrus*, p. 250). Shula may lack the moral vocabulary to express this insight in anything but selfish terms and the other characters may miss it by looking at it from very different positions. Her love is likely to be a mixture of selfishness and selflessness. She may be attracted to the Good at some cost to actual individuals. Yet, none of this implies that she did not also retrieve a genuine memory of what is essential in our lives. Love is ambiguous. It is often, but not always, selfish. It is also central to our lives and it motivates us. As Murdoch puts it: '... we are spiritual creatures, attracted by excellence and made for the Good' (Murdoch, 2001, p. 100). This remembered attraction to the Good explains why Shula refuses to compromise any longer and why she fears that if she stays with Alistair, her love may attach itself to something unworthy, she will start to hate Alistair, or all love will be crushed out of her. Turning 60 (as Shula does in the summer of 2018) is not a reason for her to give up on loving. On the contrary, there is no retirement age in moral pilgrimage.

This explanation has by necessity brushed over distinctions. I don't expect to have convinced Shula's many detractors. However, I do hope to have shown a perspective that has been largely neglected. If any of my argument holds, the best option for Shula and Alistair out of their horrid passive-aggressive exchanges is to tend to something they both love, as they do at one moment of respite when attending her horse, Sintra (BBC Radio 4g). The love for this horse made both their worlds shift away from their own concerns, even if only for a brief moment. Love is fundamental for our well-being and needs our constant care, while acknowledging that there are also times when one simply has to pay the bills (Murdoch, 2001, p. 41). Or we may hope that Shula, on one of her visits to Felpersham cathedral, will run into the abbess of Imber, a character from Murdoch's fourth novel *The Bell*, whom Murdoch was said to resemble (Murdoch, 1958; cp. Wilson, 2003, p. 177; Leeson, 2010, p. 103). What dialogue may ensue, what moral vocabulary and visions would be exchanged, I have occasionally wondered.

REFERENCES

BBC Radio 4(a). (2018, June 14). *The Archers*. Retrieved from https://www.bbc.co.uk/programmes/b0b5x388. Accessed on 28 October 2018.

BBC Radio 4(b). (2018, March 14). *The Archers*. Retrieved from https://www.bbc.co.uk/programmes/b09v6xx1. Accessed on 28 October 2018.

BBC Radio 4(c). (2018, March 15). *The Archers*. Retrieved from https://www.bbc.co.uk/programmes/b09v8m79. Accessed on 28 October 2018.

BBC Radio 4(d). (2018, March 18). *The Archers*. Retrieved from https://www.bbc.co.uk/programmes/ b09vzg85. Accessed on 28 October 2018.

BBC Radio 4(e). (2018, April 2). *The Archers*. Retrieved from https://www.bbc.co.uk/programmes/b09xjg3y. Accessed on 28 October 2018.

BBC Radio 4(f). (2018, April 22). *The Archers*. Retrieved from https://www.bbc.co.uk/programmes/b0bfz5k0. Accessed on 28 October 2018.

BBC Radio 4(g). (2018, April 26). *The Archers*. Retrieved from https://www.bbc.co.uk/programmes/b0bgbpsl. Accessed on 28 October 2018.

BBC Radio 4(h). (2018, April 6). *The Archers*. Retrieved from https://www.bbc.co.uk/programmes/b09xp2gc. Accessed on 28 October 2018.

Hopwood, M. (2018). "The extremely difficult realization that something other than oneself is real": Iris Murdoch on love and moral agency. *European Journal of Philosophy*, *26*(1), 477–501.

Leeson, M. (2010). *Iris Murdoch: Philosophical novelist*. London: Continuum.

Merritt, M. M. (2017). Love, respect, and individuals: Murdoch as a guide to Kantian Ethics. *European Journal of Philosophy*, *25*(4), 1844–1863.

Murdoch, I. (1958). *The Bell*. London: Chatto & Windus.

Murdoch, I. (1993). *Metaphysics as a guide to morals*. Hardmondsworth: Penguin.

Murdoch, I. (1997). *Existentialists and mystics: Writings on philosophy and literature*. London: Chatto & Windus.

Murdoch, I. (2001). *The sovereignty of good*. London: Routledge.

Nussbaum, M. C. (2012). "Faint with secret knowledge": Love and vision in Murdoch's the black prince. In J. Broackes (ed.), *Iris Murdoch, philosopher*, (pp. 135–153). Oxford: Oxford University Press.

Plato. (2009). *Phaedrus* [Translated with an introduction and notes by Waterfield, R.]. Oxford: Oxford University Press.

Vlastos, G. (1973). The individual as an object of love in Plato. In *Platonic studies*. Princeton, NJ: Princeton University Press.

Warnock, M. (2002). *A memoir: People and places*. London: Duckbacks.

Wilson, A. N. (2003). *Iris Murdoch as I knew her*. London: Hutchinson.

8

OH BABY! UNPLANNED PREGNANCY AND A WOMAN'S RIGHT TO CHOOSE

Carolynne Henshaw

ABSTRACT

This chapter asks, how do the decisions made by Ambridge women compare to the rest of the UK when faced with an unexpected positive pregnancy test, and will explore the decisions made by four Ambridge women when faced with the question of their own pregnancies. It will firstly present the UK context of pregnancy and family composition and go on to examine four case studies of unplanned pregnancy, the decision-making process encountered and its outcomes in BBC Radio 4's The Archers.

THE UK CONTEXT

Around one in six pregnancies in the UK are unplanned, although a further 29% are, in the terms of a study published in *The Lancet*, considered 'ambivalent', leaving only 55% of

UK pregnancies as fully intended events (Wellings et al., 2013). According to the *Lancet* study only 5.7% of unplanned pregnancies go to term, with 57.1% ending in abortion and another 33.6% in miscarriage. For those pregnancies classed as ambivalent in the study, only 28% make it to full term (Wellings et al., 2013). In the UK, one in three women will experience abortion in their lifetime. It was decriminalised in limited circumstances in 1967 (Legislation.gov.uk). It is also worth considering in the context of Ambridge that there are significant differences in the pregnancy rates between rural and urban populations with rural and small town fertility in 2011 varying between 2.2 and 2.3%, while at the same time, city and large town populations saw a fertility rate of between 1.9 and 1.95% (Rutter, 1989). The factors resulting in this difference are complex and not well documented. This makes cause and correlation hard to argue, with a number of demographic variables at play, including education, relationship, career, age and ethnicity in addition to the rural or urban setting. According to the Office for National Statistics (ONS), it's most common for women to start a family in their early 30s (ONS, 2016a) and in 2016, 84% of babies were registered by parents who were married, in a civil partnership or cohabiting. This statistic has remained unchanged since 2003. Families are getting smaller from generation to generation, with an average of 1.91 children for the 1971 cohort falling from 2.21 for the 1944 cohort (ONS, 2016b). Childbearing at older ages increases while teenage childbearing falls.

THE AMBRIDGE SITUATION

Since *The Archers*' inception there have been approximately a dozen storylines pertaining to unplanned and/or unwanted pregnancy (BBC Radio, n.d.), from Jennifer Archer's pregnancy with Adam (Macy) in 1966, through to the birth of Pip Archer's daughter Rosie (Archer) in 2018. Two of these storylines have ended in abortion and two in miscarriages. This chapter follows four of these pregnancy storylines, where three of the Ambridge women decided to progress with their pregnancies, after initially considering a termination, whilst the fourth did the opposite. Does this behaviour and decision-making reflect decisions made by other women in the UK in the same position or do Ambridge women make different choices? Is it even fair to extrapolate?

Unexpected pregnancy yields different reactions in *The Archers*, just as it does in real life. Susan (then) Horrobin's pregnancy with Emma (Carter/Grundy) expedited a marriage proposal from Neil Carter. Kate Aldridge decided not to take mum Jennifer's advice about having an abortion, and instead – somewhat infamously – gave birth to Phoebe (Aldridge) in a tent in Glastonbury (Episode, 28 June 1998). Tom Archer and Kirsty Miller's night of passion in 2017 ultimately ended in a miscarriage, after turning their worlds upside down for a second time after Tom spectacularly ditched Kirsty at the altar in 2014 (BBC Radio 4a).

Case Study 1 – Helen Archer

Helen Archer became pregnant as a result of marital rape by her then husband and serial abuser Rob Titchener. Helen said this of the ordeal when she was in court, defending the charges of attempted murder and wounding with intent:

> Rob, he was determined to have a baby. I told him I wasn't ready but he wouldn't listen. The first time he plied me with wine he held me down by my wrists. I told myself, he was my husband, it should be fine, but

it wasn't fine, was it. Mum, Dad, I'm so sorry. Rob
raped me. Not just once. It happened over and over
again *(BBC Radio 4c)*.

Rob and Helen's relationship was the subject of an often
harrowing coercive control storyline that ran for more than
two years and included scenes of physical and psychological
violence. The storyline climaxed with a heavily pregnant
Helen stabbing Rob in the heat of an argument and provoked
specifically when she thought her son, Henry, was at risk of
being harmed after he got out of bed to find out why there was
shouting in the kitchen (BBC Radio 4b). For women experiencing intimate partner violence, being killed by a partner, or
committing suicide, is a sadly more common end (World
Health Organisation and Pan American Health Organization,
n.d.). For a moment, it seemed that this might be what the
scriptwriters had in mind when Rob put a kitchen knife in
Helen's hand and implied that the only way he would ever let
her leave is if she killed herself. It's easy to see why the idea of
killing off one of their main characters would have been
unattractive, and they instead looked for a story arc that kept
Helen in Ambridge. *The Archers* editor Sean O'Connor said at
the time:

> I was very keen that having accompanied Helen on
> every step of her painful story, there would be hope
> for her and her future. We know that life isn't always
> like that but sometimes drama can and needs to offer
> us a sense of redemption. That's why we decided to
> conclude the trial with the verdict that we did
> (Slawson, 2016).

But what about her decision to keep baby Jack? Is that in
keeping with reality? Whilst it's all but impossible to get exact
statistics on the number of pregnancies carried to full term

that have resulted from marital rape, due to the nature of this violence, there have been a number of studies carried out on users of healthcare and refuge services. We know from women's testimony that pregnancy coercion exists, and there is good evidence that there is a link between intimate partner violence and unintended pregnancy, and 'the risk for unintended pregnancy doubled among those women reporting both partner violence and reproductive coercion' (Miller et al., 2010). Thus, it can be considered realistic that Helen's decision to have Jack was in line with an expected outcome for a woman in her situation. Furthermore, in devising, writing and delivering the storyline to ensure its accuracy in fact and tone, the scriptwriters worked with the charities Refuge and Woman's Aid on the story's development and Louise Patikas, who plays Helen, and also met with survivors of domestic violence (Slawson, 2016). The storyline was widely praised by survivors and charities alike for being both realistic and well handled and helping to raise awareness of an important issue. One listener, Paul Trueman, even went so far as to set up *The Helen Titchener (nee Archer) Rescue Fund* (JustGiving.com), which at the time of writing, had raised £173,235 for Refuge, a UK charity providing specialist support for women and children experiencing domestic violence.

Case Study 2 – Pip Archer

Pip Archer fell pregnant, aged 24, after a condom failed during a post breakup hookup with Toby Fairbrother. This storyline thus includes issues of contraception failure, unplanned pregnancy, younger age pregnancy and pregnancy outside of marriage.

What do the UK statistical norms tell us of Pip's situation and her course of action against this norm? With typical use, condoms are around 82% effective; around 18 in 100 women will get pregnant in a year for this reason (Family Planning Association, 2017). Thus, to become pregnant whilst using condoms as the sole means of contraception is a fairly commonplace occurrence. One in six pregnancies among women in Britain is unplanned (Wellcome, 2013), and there has been a long-term rise in the percentage of conceptions occurring outside marriage or civil partnership, reaching 58% in 2016 in England and Wales (ONS, 2016c). According to the ONS, 31.6% of Pip's peers aged 20–24 choose to terminate their pregnancies (ONS, 2016c). Thus, Pip's decision to continue the pregnancy and have Rosie seems to be roughly in line with her age cohort. This is further affirmed when taking into account the *Lancet* study that finds 57.1% of unwanted pregnancies are aborted (Wellings et al., 2013).

Case Study 3 – Vicky Tucker

Vicky Tucker was shocked to find herself pregnant in her late 40s, and subsequently discovered the child would have Down's syndrome. Her husband Mike Tucker was heading towards his 60s and retirement and voiced concerns that they would struggle to cope with a child with additional and unknown needs. Vicky, on the other hand, was always determined to keep the pregnancy as this was her first and (she felt) possibly only opportunity to become a mother. The emotive storyline was handled with sensitivity by *The Archers* scriptwriters and accurately reflected the soul-searching that forms part of the decision-making process. However, the BBC can be rightly criticised with its attempts to engage listeners in the storyline with a notorious and crude poll that asked them to vote on Vicky's decision with a simplistic yes/no outcome. This was called to account by Jane Fisher, from Antenatal

Results and Choices, one of the charities that supports expectant and bereaved parents (Revior & Thomas, 2012).

When trying to determine whether Vicky and Mike's choice reflects the national average, we are fortunate to have extremely accurate statistics for pregnancies where Down's syndrome is diagnosed. All pregnant women are offered optional antenatal screening on the NHS, and one of the screened conditions is Down's syndrome. There is also reliable data on the number of terminations related to these pregnancies in The National Down Syndrome Cytogenetic Register for England and Wales. The register shows that Vicky and Mike's decision to keep Bethany was mirrored by just 9% (1989–2011) of parents faced with a similar screening result. Parents have said that it is a particularly agonising decision (Antenatal Results and Choices, n.d.) to make because the condition can present with a wide range of symptoms. It is impossible to know prenatally exactly what needs the child will have. Whilst Vicky was very quickly certain that she wanted to continue with the pregnancy, Mike wrestled with what the impact might be on their lives. Vicky eventually won him over. Bethany's needs seem to be at the lower end of the spectrum, and the joy that she has brought to Mike and Vicky's lives is evident. We may not get to hear much about Bethany's childhood as the Tuckers moved away from Ambridge in order to get Bethany a place in a school that could provide her with this specialist support.

Case Study 4 – Elizabeth Pargetter (Then, Archer)

Twenty-four-year-old Elizabeth (then) Archer chose to have an abortion after the breakdown of her relationship with conman Cameron Fraser in 1992. Elizabeth's storyline is one of a naive young woman dating a mendacious and unreliable older man. The storyline began when Cameron Fraser bought the Berrow Farm Estate in 1990. Elizabeth pursued him persistently, despite his relationship with Caroline Bone (later, Sterling). However, even after they started a sexual relationship the 'love' was clearly one-sided, as sister Shula (then, Hebden, now Hebden Lloyd) suspected. Around seven months into the relationship when Elizabeth started feeling sick, Debbie Aldridge took her to a chemist to take a pregnancy test, which was positive. Her mother and father were supportive and encouraged her to keep the baby and dump the man. At the same time, her boss Nigel Pargetter's kindness and evident romantic interest in her confused Elizabeth still further. Cameron, far from being delighted at the news he was to become a father, coolly offered to pay for an abortion, which Elizabeth was initially unable to countenance. Eventually, Cameron announced that he and Elizabeth were going away on a mystery trip, but in a dramatic turn of events he abandoned her in a car park on the M40, the holiday having been a ruse for a flit from his creditors. Devastated, Elizabeth returned to Ambridge where Shula offered to adopt the child, whose attempts to have a baby with husband Mark Hebden had proved unsuccessful (Miller, 2015). Nevertheless, despite Shula's offer and her mother's protests, Elizabeth disappeared and had an abortion in a clinic in Felpersham. When she returned to Ambridge she told her shocked parents that after much soul-searching, she 'just couldn't have the baby' (@BBCTheArchers, 2017).

Under the current legal framework in the UK, Elizabeth's abortion would likely have been carried out under 'ground C', where the pregnancy has not exceeded the 24th week and continuance of pregnancy would involve risk, greater than if the pregnancy were terminated, of injury to the physical or mental health of the pregnancy woman. The majority (97%) of abortions are undertaken under ground C, and the majority of those (99.8%) are reported as being performed because of a risk to the woman's mental health (Department of Health, 2016). No additional information is currently required to be collected about these women, and so we only have anecdotal information as to the widely varied circumstances which lead them to seek an abortion. Elizabeth's story is certainly dramatic – this storyline makes its way onto many lists of the soap's most shocking storylines (Collins, 2011) – but is by no means any more shocking than many of the real-life stories that doctors witness throughout their careers (Royal College of Obstetricians and Gynaecologists, 2017).

CONCLUSION

So, do the women of Ambridge behave 'normally' when faced with an unexpected pregnancy? With such a small catchment area and limited demographic information it's hard to extrapolate. On the one hand, there have only been two known abortions in Ambridge since abortion legalisation in 1967. This seems an unusually low number. Looking at the national statistics, it seems very likely that over the years several Ambridge women have gone to Felpersham 'shopping' or up to London 'to visit a friend'. On the other hand, abortion stigma still exists in the UK (Purcell, Hilton, & McDaid, 2017), and the majority of people tend to keep their decisions under wraps, telling perhaps only a few close friends or family members, and possibly the father. Thus, it may be that the scriptwriters are telling us only the stories that are more widely known in the village – and that Sabrina Thwaite, Carol Treggoran, Lynda Snell and perhaps even the Button girls all have stories to tell that have eluded both Susan's hungry ears and our own.

REFERENCES

@BBCTheArchers. (2017, December 3). *This is the heart-breaking reason why Elizabeth is the only person Pip can talk to #thearchers.* Twitter, 7:15 pm. Retrieved from https://twitter.com/bbcthearchers/status/937399918322438144?lang=en. Accessed on 27 October 2018.

Antenatal Results and Choices. (n.d.). *The burden of choice.* Retrieved from https://www.arc-uk.org/for-parents/publications-2/burden-of-choice-2. Accessed on 27 October 2018.

BBC Radio 4. (n.d.). *A short history of unplanned pregnancies in Ambridge.* Retrieved from http://www.bbc.co.uk/programmes/articles/1qNsLm77mMbhs9vcbFSGYF5/a-short-history-of-unplanned-pregnancies-in-ambridge. Accessed on 27 October 2018.

BBC Radio 4(a). (2014, April 24). *The Archers.* Retrieved from https://www.bbc.co.uk/programmes/b0418rct. Accessed on 28 October 2018.

BBC Radio 4(b). (2016, April 3). *The Archers.* Retrieved from https://www.bbc.co.uk/programmes/b075mmqr. Accessed on 28 October 2018.

BBC Radio 4(c). (2016, September 6). *The Archers.* Retrieved from https://www.bbc.co.uk/programmes/b07sy5yg. Accessed on 28 October 2018.

Collins, N. (2011, January 2). The Archers: Most shocking storylines. *The Telegraph.* Retrieved from https://www.telegraph.co.uk/culture/tvandradio/bbc/8236576/The-Archers-most-shocking-storylines.html. Accessed on 27 October 2018.

Department of Health. (2016). *Abortion statistics, England and Wales: 2016.* Retrieved from https://

assets.publishing.service.gov.uk/government/uploads/system/uploads/attachment_data/file/679028/Abortions_stats_England_Wales_2016.pdf. Accessed on 27 October 2018.

Family Planning Association. (2017). *Your guide to contraception*. Retrieved from https://www.fpa.org.uk/sites/default/files/your-guide-to-contraception.pdf. Accessed on 27 October 2018.

JustGiving.com. *The Helen Titchener (nee Archer) Rescue Fund*. Retrieved from https://www.justgiving.com/fundraising/helentitchener. Accessed on 27 October 2018.

Legislation.gov.uk. *Abortion Act 1967*. Retrieved from https://www.legislation.gov.uk/ukpga/1967/87/contents. Accessed on 27 October 2018.

Miller, B. (2015). *For the love of The Archers*. Chichester: Summersdale.

Miller, E., et al (2010, April). Pregnancy coercion, intimate partner violence and unintended pregnancy. *Contraception*, *81*(4), 316–322. Retrieved from https://www.contraceptionjournal.org/article/S0010-7824(09)00522-8/abstract. Accessed on 27 October 2018.

Office for National Statistics. (2016a). *Statistical bulletin: Births by parents' characteristics in England and Wales: 2016*. Retrieved from https://www.ons.gov.uk/peoplepopulationandcommunity/birthsdeathsandmarriages/livebirths/bulletins/birthsbyparentscharacteristicsinenglandandwales/2016#average-ages-of-mothers-and-fathers-have-continued-to-rise. Accessed on 27 October 2018.

Office for National Statistics. (2016b). *Statistical bulletin: Childbearing for women born in different years, England and Wales: 2016*. Retrieved from https://www.ons.gov.uk/peoplepopulationandcommunity/birthsdeathsandmarriages/

conceptionandfertilityrates/bulletins/childbearingforwomen
bornindifferentyearsenglandandwales/2016. Accessed on 27
October 2018.

Office for National Statistics. (2016c). *Statistical bulletin:
Conceptions in England and Wales: 2016*. Retrieved from
https://www.ons.gov.uk/peoplepopulationandcommunity/
birthsdeathsandmarriages/conceptionandfertilityrates/bulle-
tins/conceptionstatistics/2016#most-conceptions-occurred-
outside-marriage-or-civil-partnership. Accessed on 27
October 2018.

Purcell, C., Hilton, S., & McDaid, L. (2017). The stigmatisation of abortion: A qualitative analysis of print media in
Great Britain in 2010. *Culture, Health & Sexuality, 16*(9),
1141–1155. Retrieved from https://www.tandfonline.com/
doi/full/10.1080/13691058.2014.937463. Accessed on 27
October 2018.

Revior, P., & Thomas, C. (2012, September 11). *Archers
producers accused of 'trivialising abortion' with online poll
on whether middle-aged couple should terminate their
Down's baby' in Mail Online*. Retrieved from http://
www.dailymail.co.uk/news/article-2201830/The-Archers-
Radio-4-accused-trivialising-abortion.html. Accessed on
27 October 2018.

Royal College of Obstetricians and Gynaecologists. (2017).
ISAD 2017 interview: Dr Kate Guthrie. Retrieved from
https://www.rcog.org.uk/en/global-network/global-health-
advocacy/international-safe-abortion-day/kate-guthrie/.
Accessed on 27 October 2018.

Rutter, M. (1989). Pathways from childhood to adult life. *The
Journal of Child Psychology and Psychiatry, 30*(1), 23–51.
Retrieved   from   https://onlinelibrary.wiley.com/doi/abs/

10.1111/j.1469-7610.1989.tb00768.x. Accessed on 27 October 2018.

Slawson, N. (2016, September 12). *The Archers' verdict on Helen Titchener concludes storyline that gripped the UK' in The Guardian.* Retrieved from https://www.the-guardian.com/tv-and-radio/2016/sep/11/the-archers-ver-dict-on-helen-tichener-aired. Accessed on 27 October 2018.

Wellcome. (2013, November 26). *One in six pregnancies among women in Britain are unplanned.* Retrieved from https://wellcome.ac.uk/press-release/one-six-pregnancies-among-women-britain-are-unplanned. Accessed on 27 October 2018.

Wellings, K., Jones, K. G., Mercer, C. H., Tanton, C., Clifton, S., Datta, J., Copas, A. J., Erens, B., Gibson, L. J., Macdowall, W., Sonnenberg, P., Phelps, A., Johnson, A. M. (2013, 30 November–6 December). The prevalence of unplanned pregnancy and associated factors in Britain: Findings from the third National Survey of Sexual Attitudes and Lifestyles (Natsal-3). *The Lancet, 382*(9907), 1807–1816. Retrieved from https://www.sciencedirect.com/science/article/pii/S0140673613620711. Accessed on 27 October 2018.

World Health Organization and Pan American Health Organization. (n.d.). *Understanding and addressing violence against women.* Retrieved from http://apps.who.int/iris/bit-stream/handle/10665/77432/WHO_RHR_12.36_eng.pdf;jsessionid=BE003164E27FB310B80545F64601CE20?sequence=1. Accessed on 27 October 2018.

9

WOMEN'S WORK?: CIVIL SOCIETY NETWORKS FOR SOCIAL STABILITY OR SOCIAL CHANGE IN AMBRIDGE

Nicola Headlam

ABSTRACT

Interrogating the networks in Ambridge can lead to a focus on kinship and familial relationships or various other forms of power and authority. This chapter focusses on the ways that civil society networks are mobilised in the village, exploring how far they are orientated towards social stability and maintenance of the status quo or towards social change. These motivations have been subjected through the collection of vignettes into an innovative social forces analysis through which the internal and external motivations of women in volunteer and informal roles are categorised as being characterised by, variously, self-reliance solidaristic activism as char-acterised by Lady Bountiful/NIMBYism and lastly benign (p)maternalism. These motivations are all seen in the high levels of subtly gendered activity undertaken in the informal realm (beyond the structures of family or contractual relationships) whereby community power can truly be viewed as a form of 'women's work'.

INTRODUCTION: AMBRIDGE: SMALL WORLD/ BIG SOCIETY?

If there are differing ways that one can use power and authority, then it follows that there are different ways to be powerful. My continued interest in the ways that power is deployed within the village of Ambridge has led me to use social network methods in order to trace who holds power and through which interactions with others they wield it. Interest in networks requires that attention be paid to the multidimensional factors concerning how people interact.

Power according to this account may be wielded as numerous and overlapping forms of embodied capital (following Bourdieu, 1986). Varieties of forms of symbolic and cultural capital may be prove to be as defining as economic status as an explanatory frame for understanding differentiation within social worlds. In looking at who wields power within the village, I have explored a list of interrelated phenomena: (1) kinship, (2) contractual/employment relations, (3) formal governance roles, (4) informal governance roles, (5) information sharing, (6) problem solving, (7) intimate 'trust-based' networks, (8) strength of weak ties (Headlam, 2017a).

I dealt with the kinship networks in the village in *Custard, Culverts and Cake* (Headlam, 2017b) (although there has been significant change since then due to some highly strategic births under the tenure of (at the time of writing) *The Archers* editor, Alison Hindell, which I look at in a blog post). This chapter focusses on the role of informal governance roles in the village.

Formal and Informal Power Relations (Fig. 9.1)

Herein I focus on the informal arenas of governance which are most clearly adjacent to the formal arena. This distinction is to emphasise the voluntaristic basis of collective citizen action. It includes identity and pressure politics, activism, voluntary and community work, social movements within the as contested dynamics of 'civil society':

> ...broadly understood as the space in society where collective citizen action takes place. This notion, however, of a societal space animated by a complex set of actors, activities, interests, and values has in fact proved extremely difficult to operationalise. This

Fig. 9.1. Formal and Informal Power Relations in Ambridge.

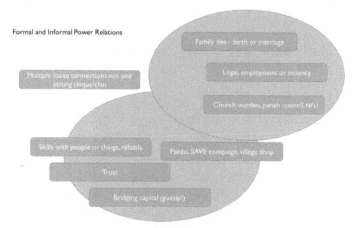

has led to a noticeable disconnection between the
theory of civil society and the practice of efforts to
support civil society; or between the abstract idea of
civil society and civil society as an observable reality.
(Malena & Heinrich, 2007)

Civil society is used as a goal of public policy as it can be a
black box into which everything without specific economic or
political causes and effects can be clustered. As part of a
multivariate account of power informality, soft power and the
functioning of civil society can be empirically studied through
social forces analysis or a civil society mapping using network
techniques.

Thus looking at the social forces that influence acts of
individual agency and action by using visual methods can
contribute towards understanding the ways in which
Ambridge residents deploy 'women's work' as a form of
power. This can be seen by tracing the individual women in
the village and their commitment to extracurricular activities.
There is more going on in the coordination of speedwatch
(say) or participation in amateur dramatics.

SOCIAL FORCES: INTERNAL MOTIVATIONS/ EXTERNAL OBJECTIVES

Indeed, if there is anything which makes Ambridge specifically Ambridge, then it is to be found in the fecund soil of
civil society, largely tended by the women residents. The
intangible but fundamental nature of these informal layers
make them somewhat resistant both to analysis and to
attempts to shape or frame voluntary activity. Despite this
there is a very long tradition of more formal political interventions seeking to shape the activities of civil society, most

notably recently was the Cameron government coalition's conceptualisation of the Big Society as a form of defining political ideology (see HMG, 2010). This proved highly problematic in the context of a far more defining policy goal of fiscal tightening, cuts to services and local government austerity. The Big Society became enmeshed with the outsourcing of functions hitherto provided by local authorities from taxation to volunteers.

> their Big Society rhetoric....it's very vague, and because it's vague, there are, you know, this whole localism and all this kind of twaddle, it's nothing new, it's been around for ages, it's just been, the language is different. *(Interview data, 2015)*

There is occasionally the sense that women of Ambridge, especially those higher up the social scale, may be drawing on less democratic social norms and expectations for women of property, reflecting the Victorian ideal of 'Lady Bountiful'. This, highly gendered and fascinating historical phenomenon is of 'ladies' as critical to the functioning of the status quo through charitable good works. For the Victorian landed gentry 'charity was seen as the special duty of the female sex as women's nature was more suited to perform acts of benevolence'.

> Frances Greville, Lady Warwick, critically described these often unspoken assumptions: My mother and stepfather were good to the poor, but it was always a goodness of extreme condescension. On matters of faith, politics, education and hygiene, they were convinced that those who served had no right to an opinion. ... A measure of serfdom prevailed ... in the surroundings of every country house I ever visited. ... Independence was not suffered. *(Gerard, 1987)*

Informal activities, according to this account, mobilise the gendered activities of soft power philanthro-capitalism in pursuit of the status quo. To a more democratic sensibility than one of rigorous hierarchy, it is possible to view civil society as mobilising in order to change society rather than to buttress it. This mentality can be seen to a degree from the combined granny power of Jill and Peggy, and the contrasting strategies of their more affluent (landed) offspring, Jenny and Elizabeth. It all points to class relations of a premodern type, as described by Philippa Byrne (2017). However, whilst there are traces of this visible from the landed families, there are other dynamics observable too.

> In a world where we have to be more self-reliant, it's more important than ever that we are not only self-reliant but find ways to help each other. You could call it the Big Society. You could call it cooperation. I prefer the concept of solidarity, because it is about people coming together from shared experiences and hopes rather than out of a sense of duty or philanthropy. *(Dobson, 2011, p. X)*

Solidarity as the basis of 'shared experiences and hopes' as foundation of civic action might offer routes towards social change rather than maintenance of the status quo. However, this account proposes mixed motivations, both external and internal, for the civic and voluntary good works of the women of Ambridge. Fig. 9.2 posits internal motivations along a continuum from the self-serving to the altruistic (along the x axis) with external objectives as a continuum from orientation towards social change or orientation towards maintenance of the status quo – or social stability (along the y axis). Ideal types of such motivations/objectives are expressed as a third transactional line with the social solidaristic approach at the opposite edge to the 'Lady Bountiful' approach.

Fig. 9.2. A Social Forces Analysis for the Voluntary Activities of Women of Ambridge.

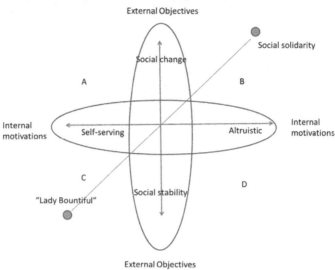

External Objectives

Social solidarity

Social change

A

B

Internal motivations

Self-serving   Altruistic

Internal motivations

C

D

"Lady Bountiful"

Social stability

External Objectives

Quadrants

(A) Self-serving motivations orientated to social change = self-reliance

(B) Altruistic motivations oriented to social change = solidaristic activism

(C) Self-serving motivations orientated towards social stability = Lady Bountiful/NIMBY

(D) Altrustic motivations orientated towards social stability = benign (p) maternalism

WOMEN'S WORK? VOLUNTEERING IN AMBRIDGE

The participation of the women of Ambridge in mobilising civil society is evidenced by their roles as membership of many overlapping groups with more or less formal status. The National Council for Voluntary Organisations (NCVO) defines volunteering as 'any activity which involves spending time, unpaid, doing something which aims to benefit someone (individuals or groups) other than or in addition to close relatives, or to benefit the environment' (The *Compact Code on Volunteering*); they find that women volunteer more than men. Twenty-eight percent of women volunteer at least once a month compared to 23% of men. Here we seek to explore the informal roles of the women of Ambridge by scrutinising their volunteering activities.

Volunteering Vignettes

Lynda Snell: Class Warrior?

Description/ Context	External Objectives/Public	Internal Motivations/Private
Lynda and Robert Snell recently commemorated their 30 years in the village with the building of a shepherd's hut representing a key pattern that has marked the British countryside in the post-war years – the in-migration of commuters and retirees into more rural locations from the suburbs of larger towns and cities.	Lynda has invested a lot in Ambridge as an **idyllic** place. As such, she has been accepted as an incomer. More recently, however, this has led to her adopting 'Not In My Back Yard' **(NIMBY)** positioning. The am-dram ructions inflicted on the village by the village panto are linked with Lynda's artistic pretensions.	There is an extensive literature on **rural gentrification** and the impact of in-movers such as the Snells. Matthews (2017) concentrates on the impact of these **in-movers** on what we might term the civic and associational life of Ambridge collective actions that helped shape the place and community.

Pat at The Elms: Offsetting Guilt?

Description/Context	External Objectives	Internal Motivations
Beginning on Christmas Day 2017, Pat and Helen Archer volunteered at local homeless shelter, The Elms. Pat continued to volunteer throughout 2018 and invited an old **activist** friend, Olwen, to stay at Bridge Farm. This coincided with the decision to sell some of Bridge Farm to Justin Elliott for housing and there was conflict between Olwen and the children of Bridge Farm, particularly Helen.	The Elms is a venue for beyond-Ambridge volunteering. It is set up as a traditional 'soup kitchen'-type day centre. Support for most vulnerable rough sleeping population admirable however, the Pat/Olwen relationship raised ethical questions about safeguarding and **appropriate boundaries.** Pat felt the need to 'save' Olwen, but Olwen served to remind Pat of her compromised values.	Pat used to be an organic farming firebrand, linking food production, **environmentalism and second-wave feminism**. She demonstrated at Greenham Common, so we assume some youthful left-radicalism as formative experiences. Since the Helen and Rob storyline, Pat has seemed unsure of herself. She has reproached herself for failing to see Rob for what he was.

Boudicca of Borsetshire: PR for Jennifer's Personal Brand?

Description/Context	External Objectives	Internal Motivations
Jenny has many avenues for unpaid work as she has never had to engage in paid work beyond	The anti-Route B SAVE campaign had many of the features of NIMBY mobilisation. It was	Except in her interactions with Debbie which are far more honest, Jennifer projects and

(Continued)

Description/Context	External Objectives	Internal Motivations
the home. She conforms to the 'Lady Bountiful' stereotype (especially as regards Will Grundy and family) which is why the storyline about her losing 'the Albion kitchen' and 'her' Home Farm has been so fraught. As village archivist and with responsibility for the village website, she has been accused of only posting news that she considers to be **appropriate**.	set up along **conventional** lines to block development and connected **upstanding** members of the community. The SAVE campaign was highly savvy in its use of local media, who portrayed her as the Boudicca of Borsetshire. The attention and flattery was an agreeable by-product for Jenny, as was the **envy** it engendered.	performs being a domestic goddess and her endless **social climbing** party organisation where she seeks to upgrade the social expectations of her relations are cringeworthy. Some of the tensions between Susan and Jennifer are overtly **class-based**.

Kirsty, Eco-activist

Description/Context	External Objectives	Internal Motivations
Kirsty has been the most committed **counter-cultural activist** in Ambridge as her environmental and social concerns	As a deep green environmentalist, Kirsty is sickened by local environmental damage, hunting, intensive farming and	Activism serves to offer an identity for Kirsty. Some find her overly oppositional in her challenge to rural practices but she

(Continued)

Description/Context	External Objectives	Internal Motivations
are a strong core of her character. Where she has operated beyond the law in destroying GM crops, she more usually demonstrates or protests legally – she has a wide range of issues of concern.	rural poverty; her finding the dead fish in the Am ensured that this would be widely known about.	remains popular with the younger people in the village. She is quite emotional and passionate about such causes and often enlists others. It was her volunteering with the food exchange café that radicalised Jill recently.

Emma's Affordable Housing Campaign

Description/Context	External Objectives	Internal Motivations
Emma Grundy has come to view her lack of house as the key to her life chances. She has lived with both her parents and her in-laws and is now highly focussed on the getting together of a deposit and in being deemed socially acceptable as a	Emma understands that there are structural, social and economic forces in play in the housing crisis, but this sometimes manifests itself as envy or resentment against her peers more able to rely on 'the bank of mum and dad', or the	Emma has made no secret that she wants an affordable house in the village in which she grew up. Her recent election to the Parish Council may risk her having a pecuniary and prejudicial interest in planning matters, which would cover the

(Continued)

Description/Context	External Objectives	Internal Motivations
candidate for shared ownership.	'Ambridge (Housing) Fairy'. She seeks to change the system for 'people like us' priced out of the housing market.	new housing development (Christened Elliottville by Academic Archers Research Fellows).

Discussion

Plotting the various positions according to this analysis does serve to expose how far motivations of the women of Ambridge are nuanced and shown from various perspectives. Insofar as their public and private motivations and objectives can be inferred, I have sought to plot them along the social force analysis designed above. Of course, this is a heuristic device to explore the dimensions in play (Fig. 9.3).

Following from the vignettes and applying the analysis to the social forces grid I do not categorise any action as 'altruism in pursuit of social stability' on display.

I have categorised Emma as displaying 'Self-serving motivations orientated to social change = self-reliance' (A). Her actions are different to those of Kirsty. Meanwhile, among those seeking social change of various types, Kirsty's environmentalism is of a more altruistic character than Emma's affordable housing campaign through which she seeks to benefit herself.

(B) Altruistic motivations oriented to social change = solidaristic activism

Kirsty is an outlier within the quadrant of social solidarity, but as her objectives are somewhat ill-defined it is hard

Fig. 9.3. Results: A Social Forces Analysis for the Voluntary Activities of Women of Ambridge.

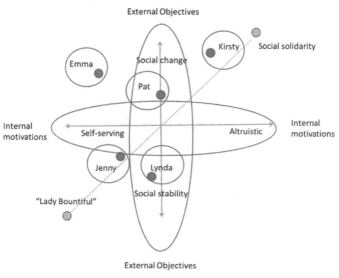

to imagine her environmentalist identity being an effective strategy.

(C) Self-serving motivations orientated towards social stability = Lady Bountiful/NIMBY

Both Jenny and Lynda, in seeking to secure continuity and stability for the village veer toward the self-serving end of the continuum. Matthews (2017) wrote extensively on the mixed meanings ascribed to Lynda in her approach to the village in his chapter in The Archers in Fact and Fiction (Courage et al, 2017). He situates her repertoire of action firmly within the tradition of middle-class *arriviste* rural gentrifiers in his seminal work *Lynda Snell: Class Warrior* (2017). She certainly toys with the possibility of retreating from public life but seems unable to do so permanently.

There are significant social benefits and prestige to her public persona (as the regular meltdowns over panto matters show every year). Jennifer does appear to use the village as an extension of her social life. She is firmly on the side of keeping things the same and policing a specific version of the past rather than engendering change. Pat's motivations in her ill-starred engagement at The Elms are harder to classify. She wants the world to be different but has suffered a loss of confidence around how that can be achieved. It is interesting to situate her well-meaning attempts to improve things in the context of her as an empty-nest baby boomer (albeit one likely to be living in a blended family with Helen, Henry and Jack for the foreseeable) she has time and resources to spare. She was more interested in social/structural change in her youth and is struggling to articulate a politics with which she is comfortable as her baby boomer asset-based affluence cushions her materially.

CONCLUSION

In conclusion, this social power analysis is one dimension of the power relations wherein Ambridge functions as a series of highly interconnected small worlds. I am preoccupied by the forms of networked social and cultural capital operating within the village of Ambridge (Headlam, 2017a, 2017b, 2018) and their role in underpinning the social interactions which keep the village functioning. Within 'soft power' networks of talk (see Chapters 3 and 4) and through their unpaid and community-based voluntary work, women are visible and active in informal contexts. Indeed, I would argue that it is in these networks and circuits that the women of Ambridge most clearly shape village life beyond their homes. The different characters, however, through their many and varied civil society roles, exert their soft power for various motives and with varying amounts of success. Their internal motivations run from overtly altruistic to self-serving and they act in pursuit of maintenance or challenge to the status quo. However, I wait with bated breath to see how far Emma is able to storm the hitherto male bastions of the formal authority of the village, using the parish council as the springboard for a political career. Using her life experience of gender and class discrimination, she can work in a more formal environment towards social change around affordable housing. We hope that she is able to move beyond the 'women's work' offered her towards exercising the levers of hard power. Further initiatives to strengthen civil society circuits and informal power in Ambridge will need to take these multifaceted public and personal motivations seriously.

REFERENCES

Bourdieu, P. (1986). Forms of cap. In J. Richardson (Ed.), *Handbook of theory and research for the sociology of education* (pp. 241–258). Westport, CT: Greenwood.

Byrne, P. (2017). The medieval world of The Archers, William Morris and the problem with class struggle (Philippa Byrne). In C. Courage, N. Headlam & P. Matthews (Eds.), *The Archers in fact and fiction: Academic analyses of life in rural Borsetshire* (p. viii). Oxford: Peter Lang.

Courage, C., Healdma, N., & Matthews, P. (2017). *The Archers in fact and fiction: Academic analyses of life in rural Borsetshire*. Oxford: Peter Lang.

Dobson, (2011). Quoted at https://www.slideshare.net/3sectorrc/decoupling-the-state-and-the-third-sector-rob-macmilla.

Gerard, J. (1987). Lady bountiful: Women of the landed classes and rural philanthropy. *Victorian Studies, 30*(2), 183–210.

Headlam, N. (2017a). Kinship networks in Ambridge. In C. Courage & N. Headlam (Eds.), *Custard, culverts and cake: Academics on life in The Archers* (pp. 191–209). Bingley: Emerald Publishing.

Headlam, N. (2017b). *Can you catch the perpetrator of a hit-and-run in an ego-net? Academic archers blogspot.* Retrieved from https://static1.squarespace.com/static/589f1e875016e176237213e1/t/59fc7bdd0846652dc5c094e9/1509719008189/egonet+matt+blog.pdf.

Headlam, N. (2018). *The Tribes of Peggy and Jill academic archers blogspot.* Retrieved from https://static1.squarespace.com/static/589f1e875016e176237213e1/t/5a721adcc83025b87bb0c983/1517427427404/peggy+jill+2018+blog+final.pdf.

HMG. (2010). *Building a Big society.* Retrieved from https://assets.publishing.service.gov.uk/government/.../building-big-society.pdf.

Malena, C., & Heinrich, V. F. (2007). Can we measure civil society? A proposed methodology for international comparative research. *Development in Practice, 17*(3), 338–352.

Matthews, P. (2017). Lynda Snell, Class Warrior: Social class and community activism in rural Borsetshire. In C. Courage, N. Headlam & P.Matthews (Eds.), *The Archers in fact and fiction: Academic analyses of life in rural Borsetshire* (p. viii). Oxford: Peter Lang.

10

STRONG OR SILENCED? THE UNDER-REPRESENTATION OF MENTAL HEALTH PROBLEMS IN AMBRIDGE'S WOMEN

Elizabeth Campion

ABSTRACT

This chapter will argue that the representation of mental illness in The Archers *is unrepresentative in a number of ways. Sufferers of long-term mental health problems are not portrayed in the programme and mental illness is often used as a narrative device, leading to a bias towards circumstantial, single-episode mental ill health storylines. This chapter will also cover the portrayal of Helen Archer's mental health during and after suffering emotional and physical abuse at the hands of her ex-husband, arguing that it suffers from a number of shortcomings.*

INTRODUCTION

Of *The Archers'* mental illness-focussed storylines, many have concerned depression and suicide in men with fewer centred around women. However, some women have been depicted with mental health problems. For example, after the death of John Archer, his mother Pat Archer had a bout of depression, while his sister Helen Archer went on to be bereaved again after her partner's suicide and became ill with anorexia nervosa. This depiction of mental illness in Ambridge's women is unrepresentative in various ways, at least partly due to the frequent use of mental health problems as a plot device or narrative arc per se, with the depiction of Helen's anorexia during the Helen and Rob Titchener storyline, for example, having various strengths and weaknesses.

WHY IS IT IMPORTANT TO REPRESENT MENTAL HEALTH PROBLEMS ACCURATELY?

The Archers officially abandoned its educational function in 1972 (BBC Radio 4, n.d.), but accurate and inclusive representation of the issues covered by the programme, whether agricultural or otherwise, remains important. Acknowledging the programme's role in 'reflecting and shaping public attitudes towards sociopolitical issues' including disability, Runswick-Cole and Wood (2017, p. 329) have pointed out the risk that stigma and marginalisation of certain groups can be increased by poorly executed representation of their lived experience. True-to-life portrayals of various mental health problems are, on the other hand, likely to be positively received by, and benefit listeners. Terry Molloy, the actor who played Mike Tucker, recalls a listener thanking him personally for his depiction of Mike's depression, likening it to 'therapy', which allowed him to feel less alone. Similarly, there was much praise for the storyline concerning Jack Woolley's dementia and eventual death. It was described as 'accurate, sensitive, moving and just true', reflecting the experiences of many in a way that they found helpful (Moreton, 2014).

HOW ACCURATE IS *THE ARCHERS'* PORTRAYAL OF MENTAL ILLNESS OVERALL?

If, to be in line with UK population levels (Mental Health Foundation, 2016), one in five of Ambridge's residents should be portrayed as suffering from mental health problems in any one year, it could make for miserable and repetitive listening. I argue though that within the framework of the programme, however, it would be possible to be more broadly representative. For example, some of the most frequently diagnosed mental health conditions such as generalised anxiety disorder, post-traumatic stress disorder, bipolar disorder and personality disorders have apparently never occurred in Ambridge. It is true that mental health problems occur slightly less frequently in rural populations, but this could not account for the rates of under-representation seen in Ambridge (Nicholson, 2008, pp. 302–311). Furthermore, most sufferers of mental ill health in Ambridge have been adult males, whereas in fact common mental disorders are more common in women and young people, with young women at particularly high risk (Mental Health Foundation, 2016).

A further problem of under-representation arises from the way mental health problems are represented in *The Archers*. Mental illness in Ambridge generally progresses according to a typical narrative structure: symptoms appear and begin to affect the character and those around them (rising action) until a climax is reached and help is sought, and professional help generally results in complete eventual resolution of symptoms (denouement, falling action). The illness therefore provides a plot, complete with narrative tension and character development. Once the dramatic potential of this plot has been fulfilled, characters can look forward to complete recovery after what appears to be generally prompt and effective medical intervention. This means that the experiences of many sufferers, including those who deal with chronic or recurrent problems, have difficulty accessing medical treatment or are not helped by it, are going unrepresented in *The Archers*. Runswick-Cole (2016) has warned of the risk of disabilities, including mental illnesses, being used as 'narrative prostheses'. For example, Darrell Makepeace's depression was used instrumentally to develop Shula Hebden Lloyd's character, missing opportunities to highlight the many problems faced by those attempting to access treatment or using mental health services at the time. This undercuts the severity of the issue being represented, trivialising its impact on the lives of all those affected.

WHY IS THIS PROBLEM PARTICULARLY RELEVANT TO WOMEN?

As stated above, women and men suffer from mental ill health at different rates, with overall prevalence higher in women than in men in the United Kingdom with illnesses such as generalised anxiety disorder and eating disorders being disproportionately present in women (Mental Health Foundation, 2016). Hysteria and neurosis have been seen as female problems throughout history, often thought (by male doctors) to result from uncontrolled sexuality (Appignanesi, 2008, pp. 143–154). An alternative view is that the impossible demands made of women throughout history and up to the present day, combined with the frequently stifling limitations placed upon them by society along with other external factors, have proved, quite literally, to be maddening. For example, Appignanesi (2008) writes that nineteenth-century hysteria was 'the disorder that best expresses women's distress at the clashing demands and no longer tenable restrictions placed on women in the fin-de-siècle [and] the difficulties of growing up woman at a time when idealisations of the family were at odds with lived experience'.

Madness has also, however, historically been a way for women to resist conventional societal roles, gain notoriety and even accomplish various goals. Charcot's famous hysterics at the Salpêtrière asylum attained both celebrity and a certain sexual freedom (Appignanesi, 2008), and even today we watch the self-destructive spirals of female celebrities with eager enthusiasm. Meanwhile, Walker Bynum (1987) has described female saints in the mediaeval period whose behaviour (including fasting, lack of menstruation, preparation of food for others, frenetic activity and feelings of unworthiness) echoes that of today's sufferers of anorexia. These were not, at the time, regarded as symptomatic behaviours, but as 'efforts to gain power and give meaning' through the 'manipulate[ion] of physicality'. These efforts were often directed at gaining control of religious expression (e.g. in order to receive the Eucharist) or to resist marriages to which they objected. Madness has, paradoxically, both arisen from the societal constraints placed on women and functioned as a way for them to affect the world around them within those boundaries.

None of this is reflected on *The Archers*. Pat and Helen were shown becoming ill as a reaction to men around them. Pat's depression resulted from the death of her son; Helen's anorexia from the suicide of her partner and later from the abuse by her husband. Furthermore, when Pat began to recover, she stated that she felt like 'a real mother' again (*The Archers*, 9 June 2004), while Helen became determined to avoid further slipping back into food restriction when she heard that her son Henry was failing to grow as fast as expected during pregnancy (small-for-dates). Through the characters of Helen and Pat, mental illness was therefore presented as something which hindered their main purpose: the performance of their stereotypical caring role of wife and mother. It is the desire to resume this role and the motivation of love for their family which encourages women to overcome the obstacle of mental illness as part of a (very conventional) sort of redemption narrative. This makes for a heart-warming, family-friendly story, but fails to reflect the experience of women whose problems are sufficiently severe and chronic to be impossible to overcome in this way and must instead be accommodated and lived with perhaps for years or those who are unable to access treatment or support. This silence implies dismissal of such women, let alone those whose illness results from their inability to conform to societal ideals of femininity.

WAS ANOREXIA USED EFFECTIVELY IN THE HELEN AND ROB STORYLINE?

Helen Archer first fell ill with anorexia nervosa in 2005, was hospitalised and then appeared to be in remission for several years. She had a mild relapse when she was pregnant with Henry, which was resolved when she discovered he was small-for-dates, and finally a more serious relapse during her marriage to Rob and pregnancy with their son Jack. Rob and his mother Ursula Titchener appeared consciously and manipulatively to trigger and exacerbate the illness by pressing unwanted fattening food on her and making calculatedly upsetting comments about her weight and shape. Helen eventually collapsed and was taken to a doctor, who appeared to take Rob's side, becoming a recruit in his campaign of terror against his wife just as her anorexia had become his weapon. These elements conspired to undermine Helen's credibility and strip her of autonomy, independence and any trace of power.

Medland (2017), in a paper discussing the relationship between food and sexual politics in Ambridge, hypothesised that Helen's refusal to eat was a form of passive resistance against Rob. The ability to control what does and does not enter one's body, to someone who has been stripped of any other form of control over their life, must seem like an effective last line of defence, 'controlling the extent to which other people can access your brain, your heart' as the author Marya Hornbacher (1998, p. 67) has put it. However, as well as a method of resistance and a powerful literary device, anorexia nervosa is a serious psychiatric condition with an average recovery time of up to seven years and a mortality rate of 10% per decade suffered. Sufferers may begin with the illusion of control, but soon the disease will begin to control them, causing stereotypical pathological behaviours and resulting in faulty perception both of the self and the surrounding world. Wolf (1990) called it a 'prison camp'; Woolf dubbed it 'that most enfeebling of conditions' (Woolf, 2012, p. 72). What could be less helpful and more terrifying to someone who is already being gaslighted, a form of abuse which also involves a fundamental undermining of their grasp on reality and control of every aspect of their existence? Self-starvation may in the past have been an effective way for women to get what they wanted, but now the experience of a woman who is distressed, unwell or out of touch with reality, stripped of any religious or other glamorous connotation is simply that much more easily dismissed. Moreover, Helen was seen to shrug her problems off seemingly effortlessly after the departure of Rob, which not only ignores the lengthy wait for eating disorders and the damage thereby wrought on sufferers and their families (Beat Eating Disorders, 2017), but also undermines the psychological damage Rob's abuse would have wrought. In reality, abuse by intimate partners tends to cause significant mental and physical health consequences, including depression, substance abuse and development of chronic mental health problems (Coker et al., 2002, p. 260). As discussed above, showing Helen moving on so easily once the dramatic part of her story is over and the attention of the listeners is away from her might be seen as casting aspersions on survivors of domestic abuse who continue to struggle for years – or even for the rest of their lives – with the consequences of what has been done to them.

CONCLUSION

In this chapter I have argued that the *The Archers* has failed to represent various experiences of mental illness. Mental health problems in the programme are either plots in themselves or narrative devices, and no character has voiced the experience of those who cope with chronic mental health issues. This problem is particularly acute in the female characters of Ambridge, in whom mental illness has only ever been a transient obstacle to their full adoption of traditional wife and mother roles. This ignores the historical and societal contexts of mental illness in women and may even go so far as to increase the stigmatisation of those who do not fit the roles depicted in the programme.

REFERENCES

Appignanesi, L. (2008). *Mad, bad and sad: A history of women and the mind doctors from 1800 to the present.* London: Virago Press.

BBC Radio 4. (n.d.). *Frequently asked questions about The Archers.* Retrieved from http://www.bbc.co.uk/programmes/articles/5xGwGj4NgfGRJ1B2mFqg6QM/frequently-asked-questions. Accessed on 27 October 2018.

Beat Eating Disorders. (2017). *Delaying for years, denied for months: The health, emotional and financial impact on sufferers, families and the NHS of delaying treatment for eating disorders in England.* Retrieved from https://www.beateatingdisorders.org.uk/uploads/documents/2017/11/delaying-for-years-denied-for-months.pdf. Accessed on 27 October 2017.

Coker, A. L., Davis, K. E., Arias, I., Desai, S., Sanderson, M., Brandt, H. M., & Smith, P. H. (2002). Physical and mental health effects of intimate partner violence for men and women. *American Journal of Preventive Medicine, 23*(4), 260.

Hornbacher, M. (1998). *Wasted: A memoir of anorexia and bulimia.* New York, NY: Flamingo.

Medland, A. (2017). Culinary coercion: Nurturing traditional gender roles in Ambridge. In C. Courage & N. Headlam (Eds.), *Custard, culverts and cake: Academics on life in The Archers.* Emerald Publishing.

Mental Health Foundation. (2016). *Fundamental facts about mental health 2016.* Retrieved from https://www.mental-health.org.uk/publications/fundamental-facts-about-mental-health-2016. Accessed on 27 October 2018.

Moreton, C. (2014, January 14). The Archers' storyline that touched a nation. *The Telegraph*. Retrieved from https://www.telegraph.co.uk/culture/tvandradio/10580615/The-Archers-storyline-that-touched-a-nation.html. Accessed on 27 October 2018.

Nicholson, L. A. (2008). Rural mental health. *Advances in Psychiatric Treatment*, 14(4), 302–311.

Runswick-Cole, K. (2016, March 6). Why The Archers needs more disabled characters. *The Independent*. Retrieved from https://www.independent.co.uk/arts-entertainment/tv/news/why-the-archers-needs-more-disabled-characters-a6915471.html. Accessed on 27 October 2018.

Runswick-Cole, K., & Wood, R. (2017). Bag of the devil: The disablement of Rob Titchener. In C. Courage & N. Headlam (Eds.), *Custard, culverts and cake: Academics on life in The Archers*. Emerald Publishing.

Walker Bynum, C. (1987). *Holy feast and holy fast: The religious significance of food to medieval women*. Berkeley, CA: University of California Press Ltd.

Wolf, N. (1990). *The beauty myth*. London: Chatto & Windus Ltd.

Woolf, E. (2012). *An apple a day: A memoir of love and recovery from anorexia*. Chichester: Summersdale Publishers Ltd.

SECTION FOUR – GENDERED EXPECTATIONS: BEYOND THE HOME

11

'WHAT WOULD THE NEIGHBOURS SAY?': GENDER AND SEXUALITY DIVERSITY IN *THE ARCHERS*

William Pitt

ABSTRACT

This chapter discusses portrayals of attitudes towards and experiences of gender and sexuality diversity in The Archers *and discusses the role of media in shaping social change. Using existing data on attitudes across the UK, a survey was developed for* The Archers' *audience to measure listener perceptions of key character attitudes. The survey findings are compared against the UK data. Broadly, the audience perceived characters in* The Archers *as reflecting a similar attitudinal spread to the UK. However, irrespective of attitudes, within* The Archers, *there is a lack of representation of the experiences of gender diversity or alternative forms of sexuality. In conclusion, I argue* The Archers *could do more to drive social change by featuring a wider range of gender diversity and non-heteronormative queer experiences.*

INTRODUCTION

This chapter discusses the ways in which gender and sexuality diversity are portrayed in *The Archers*. Historically, gender diverse and queer people have been marginalised, at best ignored and at worst abused or killed for their differences. In the UK, social attitudes are moving from tolerance to acceptance, but there is still a way to go (Swales & Taylor, 2017). This chapter explores whether and how *The Archers* portrays gender diversity and sexuality, using an audience survey, and discusses what this means for both the programme, its audience and wider society. Social change does not happen by itself. It comes from awareness, knowledge and understanding. I argue that as a British media stalwart, *The Archers* has a role to play in pushing past tolerance and continuing to shape the acceptance of gender diverse and queer people. While social views reflect society, they are inherently individual and the personal nature of how characters are 'seen' in radio programmes makes *The Archers* a powerful medium to affect change.

GENDER DIVERSITY

Sex refers to physiological and biological characteristics of a human (Stonewall UK, 2017), most useful when looking at phenomena affected by the body, for example, testosterone influences risk-taking behaviour in young males. Gender refers to socially constructed roles, behaviours, activities and attributes. The terms *man, masculine, woman and feminine* denote gender. Gender is a spectrum inclusive of masculine and feminine identities as opposed to an often-assumed masculine/feminine binary (Stonewall UK, 2017), most interesting when considering sociocultural phenomena, such as studying barriers to women's participation in science or mathematics. Transgender people are people who are born with their gender and birth sex out of alignment (Stonewall UK, 2017). Like anybody else, they may fall anywhere on the gender spectrum and may or may not choose to 'transition' to change official documents, 'come out' to friends and family or more closely align their body or appearance with their gender, medically or otherwise.

The Fawcett Society, a charity campaigning for women's and gender equality, did a study of 8000-plus people in late 2015 looking at attitudes to gender (Fawcett Society, 2016). They found opinion on gender identity split in Britain. More than half (56%) think there are two genders and less than half (44%) think gender can be a range of identities. Women take a more fluid view than men. Forty-eight percent of women think gender can be a range of identities compared with 39% of men. Attitudes also align with age: 65% of those aged above 65 years think gender is binary, compared with 44% of 18–24 year olds, both significantly different from the national average of 56%.

The GMFA (formerly Gay Men Fighting AIDS), a charity focussing on gay men's health, did a study of 1,000-plus people between 2015 and 2016 (GMFA, 2016) looking at attitudes to gay men's open relationships. What they found is that gay men who have experience of open relationships are more open to such relationships and rate them more favourably. Gay men who have no experience of such relationships tend to be more critical of open relationships. Specifically, looking at men who believe themselves to be in a monogamous relationship with no experience of an open relationship, the study found the following: just under a fifth (18%) thought open relationships can be a good thing, while just under a third (30%) thought they can be bad for relationships; exactly a third (33%) thought them not 'real' relationships; just over half (54%) would rather be single than be in an open relationship and when considering why open relationships were prevalent among gay men, a fifth (19%) believed relationships end up open as men can't be monogamous.

THE ROLE OF THE MEDIA

Media is a powerful tool to reflect and shape social attitudes. Historically the media has been used to portray social concerns and highlight underrepresented groups, allowing minorities to draw inspiration or support from the programming. For example, a commercially successful television programme portraying homosexuality on mainstream television is widely credited as shaping positive social attitudes to homosexuality (Borden, 2017). Schiappa, Gregg, and Hewes (2006) found increased viewing of the programme reduced prejudice towards gay and lesbian people, with a greater effect among those with less social contact with gay or lesbian people. Although only recently discussed more frequently and openly, gender diversity has always existed. For example, transgender is not a new concept – there is a long history of transgender people throughout history. In recent history, it was non-gender conforming and trans (of colour) such as Marsha P Johnson and Sylvia Rivera at the Stonewall Riots who were at the forefront of the queer rights movement. More recently, there has been more representation of trans women in media with Laverne Cox famously appearing in Netflix's *Orange Is the New Black* and journalist India Willoughby appearing on popular television programme, *Celebrity Big Brother*. Including minorities in media can act as a tool to promote harmony. Movements like

#OscarsSoWhite have sparked debate in Hollywood. Films like *Black Panther* and *Moonlight* mark a paradigm shift in diversity and provide inspiration to black and queer people across the globe. This then leads to follow-on effects where wider society becomes more accepting, as with *Will and Grace* and homosexuality. Representation in media can be an important way to expose people to diverse communities, increasing acceptance, as well as being important to people within communities.

THE ROLE OF *THE ARCHERS*

Representation can give permission to people to be themselves. We have never 'seen' a character on *The Archers* but radio dramas have a special power to portray characters as they exist only in the listener's subjective mind. When listening, we see 'our' Brookfield farmhouse and 'our' Neil and Susan Carter on chilli night. *The Archers* has a history with social change, addressing topics such as GM crops, Eastern European workers, and women farmers, for example, but how does *The Archers* portray gender and sexuality diversity?

METHODOLOGY

To compare Ambridge against the UK norm, I undertook a study designed to compare characterised villager attitudes in Ambridge with those in the UK, working with questions on gender diversity and sexuality from the Fawcett and GFMA studies. With apologies to Archers Anarchists (n.d.), without being able to speak directly with villagers, I approached *The Archers* audience through an online survey as to their suppositions on Ambridge resident opinion. I first took questions from several existing UK studies that look at attitudes to gender and sexuality. I then selected a range of characters, to ensure a mix of age, gender and class, and asked the participants how they thought characters would respond to the questions. This was designed to measure the consistency audience perceptions of characters' attitudes. Fieldwork was conducted over two weeks, and participants were reached through various *The Archers* Facebook groups and Twitter. Two hundred and fourteen responses were received.

FINDINGS

When considering gender, participants attributed a range of attitudes among Ambridge residents towards the Fawcett Society's question on gender identity and held consistent views on who would think what amongst the villagers. Will Grundy, Susan, Kirsty Miller, Justin Elliott and Jill Archer had the most consistent interpretations with Ed Grundy, Jennifer Aldridge, Pat Archer and Pip Archer having slightly less consistent results and with clear skews. According to participants, Ed, Will and Justin all lean towards there being only two genders. Similarly, the older characters, Jill and Jennifer, did too. Kirsty was the outlier, definitely believing in multiple genders, with Pat and Pip likely supporting this view too. The differences by gender and age broadly align with the national results. Older characters, as with older citizens, believe there are two genders, while the women and younger characters believe there is a spectrum.

When considering gay men and open relationships, participants considered how the two openly gay men living in Ambridge, Adam Macy and Ian Craig, feel towards open relationships. They thought Adam seemed more open to open relationships than Ian. It was clear Ian considers open relationships as bad for relationships, not real relationships, and that he'd rather be single than be in an open relationship. Perceptions of Adam's attitudes were slightly different. Whilst participants thought he would think open relationships are bad for relationships (perhaps reflecting on his time in The Bull while split from Ian), and only a very small proportion thought Adam wouldn't think of open relationships as real relationships, he was considered far more likely to see open relationships as a good thing than Ian. Interpretations of Ian and Adam's position towards open relationships feel similar to gay men in the UK who, like them, do not have experience of being in an open relationship (unless there's something Adam or Ian haven't told us!).

DISCUSSION

In a follow-up study, I would propose including a wider selection of characters for each question and a possible random selection to avoid researcher bias. In this study, they were purposively selected to reflect a mix of age, gender and class to limit the number of questions and make the survey easier to complete for participants. Ideally, their response to the questions, demographic information and a fondness score for each character would also be collected. Perhaps the interpretation of art, literature and media can never be separated from the audiences' own position, but with more information, it would be possible to draw commentary on whether people read in their own views or projected onto characters they like or dislike instead of 'just' interpreting how characters are portrayed.

CONCLUSIONS

There are a range of attitudes portrayed by characters in *The Archers*, as interpreted by the audience. The diversity of attitudes appears to be reflective of the UK findings even if the diversity of experiences is not. Given the consistency in responses to the gender question, it appears the characters within *The Archers* are portraying a diversity of attitudes. But attitudes can be implicit and not always expressed. There does not appear to be any portrayal of experiences – as yet no storyline has touched on gender diversity or transgenderism. While Adam and Ian's courtship, early relationship, married life and now aiming to start a family have been documented extensively, we have not seen any deviation from a traditional, heteronormative relationship. Adam has had a few 'encounters' with other men (it is a soap!) but all without Ian's prior knowledge or consent.

We do not know of any transgender characters in *The Archers*, nobody has discussed a gender spectrum and transgender rates are substantially lower in Ambridge than nationally. One might expect Ambridge as a small village in a rural area to not have many minority residents, given skews to urban areas. However, one should not accept that in Ambridge, the epicentre of *The Archers,* expecting characters to reflect the diversity of experiences across the UK is too much to ask. *The Archers* is well placed to drive social change. With its prominence, comes a responsibility in telling stories about the UK experience to reflect the diversity of its reality. Expressions of non-traditional relationships among queer and straight people in Ambridge could open a renegotiation of what it means for two people to join into a relationship, as many in the UK are and do. Furthermore, a more explicit portrayal of transgender or gender diverse people in *The Archers* would help normalise gender diversity and work towards reducing transphobic prejudice. Given the audience skew to an older demographic, who generally hold more conservative views, the impact would be far greater than 'preaching to the converted' in youth media. Social change is inherently modern, creating a true to brand portrayal of contemporary drama in a rural setting.

REFERENCES

Archers Anarchists. (n.d.). *The Archers are real – There is no cast*. Retrieved from https://www.archersanarchists.com. Accessed on 26 October 2018.

Borden, J. (2017, September 14). 'Will & Grace' reduced homophobia, but can it still have an impact today? *The Washington Post*. Retrieved from https://www.washingtonpost.com/entertainment/will-and-grace-reduced-homophobia-but-can-it-still-have-an-impact-today/2017/09/14/0e6b0994-9704-11e7-82e4-f1076f6d6152_story.html?noredirect=on&utm_term=.2c78b9fe6e62. Accessed on 26 October 2018.

Fawcett Society. (2016). *Attitudes to gender study*. Retrieved from http://survation.com/uk-attitudes-to-gender-in-2016-survation-for-fawcett-society/. Accessed 26 October 2018.

Mahboubian-Jones. (2016). *Open relationships uncovered*. GMFA, London: UK. Retrieved from https://www.gmfa.org.uk/fs152-open-relationships-uncovered. Accessed on 26 October 2018.

Schiappa, E., Gregg, P. B., & Hewes, D. E. (2006). Can one TV show make a difference? Will & Grace and the para-social contact hypothesis. *Journal of Homosexuality*, *51*(4), 15–37.

Stonewall UK. (2017). *Glossary of terms*. Retrieved from https://www.stonewall.org.uk/help-advice/glossary-terms. Accessed on 26 October 2018.

Swales, K., & Taylor, E. A. (2017). *Moral issues: British social attitudes 34*. Natcen, UK. Retrieved from http://www.bsa. natcen.ac.uk/media/39147/bsa34_moral_issues_final.pdf. Accessed on 26 October 2018.

12

AMBRIDGE: KEEPING THE PIPELINE OF UK FEMALE SCIENTISTS FLOWING

Jane Turner and Clare Warren

ABSTRACT

In 1976, in a speech at Ruskin College, Oxford, Prime Minister James Callaghan asked 'Why is it that such a high proportion of girls abandon science before leaving school?' (Gillard, 2018). Little has changed over the last 40 years; a recent report from the National Audit Office (2018, p. 28) stated that only 8% of science, technology, engineering and mathematics (STEM) apprenticeships were taken up by women in 2016/2017 and that the shortage of STEM skills in the workforce is a key UK economic problem. However, just as the Aldridge marriage has been the source of considerable interest and the site of significant financial investment in terms of designer kitchens and expensive holidays, so has the issue of 'girls in science' been a consistently debated topic and taken up a large chunk of government and industry spending. Research (Archer et al., 2013) suggests that although children enjoy their science experiences in school, too few pupils aspire to a STEM career. It reveals that the pupils most likely to aspire to careers in science are those whose families have high 'science capital' which 'refers to the science-related qualifications, understanding, knowledge (about science and "how it works"), interest and social contacts (e.g. "knowing someone who works in a science-related job")' (Archer et al., 2016, p. 3).

Episodes of The Archers *are full of scientific talk, from herbal leys to plate meters. This chapter looks at how the science capital in Ambridge is shared. Why is Alice Carter an engineer and not Emma Grundy? Will Kiera Grundy choose physics A level? Who are the female STEM role models? How can the concept of science capital help us to understand the career paths of Ambridge residents? Will the young girls of Ambridge remedy the gender imbalance in STEM careers?*

THE STEM SKILLS GAP

There are multiple political, social and individual reasons why girls should be encouraged to think that science is for them, but the reason that £990 million has been invested in interventions between 2007 and 2017 to address the issue of insufficient numbers of STEM professionals in the workforce (National Audit Office, 2018, p. 4) is undoubtedly more to do with economics than equity. There are simply not enough young people choosing to study STEM subjects after the age of 16 to meet the future demands of the UK economy. A 2018 survey (Stem.org.uk, 2018) revealed that 89% of STEM businesses have found it difficult to hire staff with the required skills in the last 12 months, leading to a current shortfall of over 173,000 workers – an average of 10 unfilled roles per business, costing them an estimated £1.5 billion a year in recruitment, temporary staffing, inflated salaries and additional training costs. Attempting to address the gender imbalance in the STEM workforce is a key way that government and industry have sought to plug the STEM skills gap. The Confederation of British Industry (CBI) (2015, p. 13) identifies that 'shifting the attitudes of young women in particular must be a priority as this is the group within which the drop off in interest is most acute'. Whitelegg (2015, p. 12) has 'focussed on increasing the numbers of girls not only for equity reasons, but also because the future supply issue would be solved if girls chose physics in similar numbers to boys'. Hence the plethora of campaigns targeted at all stages of education and STEM employers to increase the number of girls and women who make the decision that science is for them. Yet despite an 18% increase in the number of women doing science and mathematics A level over the last seven years, girls and women are still under-represented in most STEM subject areas at every stage of the STEM skills pipeline (House of Lords: Select Committee on Science and Technology, 2018, p. 112).

THE AMBRIDGE WOMEN'S STEM BUBBLE

However, the national picture does not seem to apply to Ambridge, where the proportion of women employed in STEM occupations in 2018 confounds the national data. A study of the BBC's *Archers* archives reveals that at the time of Callaghan's Ruskin speech there were no female characters in STEM employment, apart from those defined as 'farmers' wives', with other women earning their living as shop assistants, barmaids and hotel receptionists. Even Pat Archer, prior to her consciousness raising in the early 1980s, fitted the stereotypical mould. However, as Julie Burchill (and in Chapter 2) noted in 1980, the arrival of the first female scriptwriters in 1975 released the women of Ambridge from 'the gallons of

greengage jam old-guard male scriptwriters kept them occupied with for over twenty years' (Hendy, 2007, p. 205). But it
wasn't until the arrival of agricultural student Ruth Pritchard
(now Archer) in 1987 that the Ambridge perception of the
female on the farm really changed: 'Ruth is more likely to have
her hand in a rubber glove rather than an oven glove – thrust
up the back end of a Friesian rather than delving into an Aga
and emerging with something wholesome for supper' (Frith &
Arnot, 2010, p. 118). Thirty-one years later women in
Ambridge make up over a third of the STEM workforce in
that corner of Borsetshire, data that would surely bring a smile
to a pessimistic statistician from the Government Department
for Business, Energy and Industrial Strategy (BEIS).

An analysis of the occupations of the Ambridge employed
was carried out by coding them following the Joint Academic
Coding System (JACS) which is used by BEIS and the Higher
Education Statistics Agency (House of Lords, Select Committee
on Science and Technology, 2018, p.112). The STEM classi-
fiers are medicine and dentistry; subjects allied to medicine;
biological sciences; veterinary science, agriculture and related
subjects; physical sciences; mathematical sciences; computer
science; engineering; technologies; and architecture, building
and planning. At the time of writing, in Ambridge there are
currently four female farmers working at a managerial level
(Ruth, Pip Archer, Debbie Aldridge and Hannah Riley), a
female engineer (Alice) and six women working in food production (Helen Archer, Pat, Clarrie Grundy, Susan Carter,
Emma and Lexi Viktorova). If the definition is extended to
'thinking science is for them', Kirsty Miller with her environmental activism should also be included in this list of 'steminists'. To allow a valid comparison with recent UK statistics
for the female proportion of the STEM workforce, medical
careers cannot be included, but even when Kate Aldridge's
holistic therapies are happily omitted, and Amy Frank's

midwifery and Anisha Jayakody's veterinary practice are ignored as they no longer live in Ambridge, the statistics for female residents employed in STEM jobs show that Ambridge is ahead of the national average (Figs. 12.1 and 12.2).

Fig. 12.1. Percentages of Men and Women Employed in STEM Occupations in Ambridge, Based on Main Characters Listed on BBC *The Archers* Website August 2018 Who Are Employed.

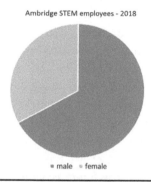

Ambridge STEM employees - 2018

■ male ■ female

Fig. 12.2. Percentages of Men and Women Employed in STEM Occupations Across the UK (WISE, 2018).

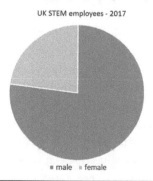

UK STEM employees - 2017

■ male ■ female

Ambridge is a farming community where generations of male farmers have passed on knowledge, affinity and experience, along with land, contracts and farming infrastructure: but until Pat and Ruth seized the tractors' steering wheels and cropping plans there were no female farmer role models to which Ambridge girls could aspire. What has happened to change the employment choices of the current generation of under 40s Ambridge farmers' daughters and their female neighbours? Is it the impact of 40-plus years of intervention and investment into women in STEM, a simple reflection of the increasing proportion of women in the UK workforce, or are there other sociological reasons? For Emma, Clarrie and Lexi the decision to work in the chicken factory or dairy is clearly driven by limited opportunities and economic need. It is widely reported that the problem of gender stereotypes is particularly persistent in STEM careers. Archer et al. (2012, p.968) 'reveal how boys exhibit more positive attitudes to science than girls do'. So what has persuaded the more advantaged women of Ambridge to pursue careers in science? Are there lessons here for policy makers, and hope for the future economic prosperity of the nation?

For many years policy has focussed on increasing the numbers of girls studying science post-16, with some success. The popularity of core STEM subjects has increased, despite the overall number of A level entries across all subjects falling. In 2018 there was a 4% increase in girls taking STEM subjects over the previous year, compared to an increase of only 0.65% for boys. 2017 saw an increase in the number of female STEM graduates (not including medical sciences) from the previous year, but women are still severely underrepresented in areas such as engineering and computing (WISE, 2018). STEM graduates Pip and Alice are still part of a UK minority, and Alice's engineering degrees classify her as a very rare specimen. However, her rarity is less remarkable in

Ambridge where the young women have a higher level of STEM qualifications than the men, bucking the national trend.

Should this be attributed to government education policy and industry campaigns or a stereotypical explanation of female academic attainment? A level subjects are rarely discussed in *The Archers* and specificities of curricula almost never; children make choices about subjects off air. Jonny Phillips's, Jamie Perk's and Chris Carter's decisions to complete apprenticeships at Borchester College were topics of discussion, as was Josh Archer's decision not to follow his sister to university to study agriculture. In these male storylines the value of academic study was considered secondary to first-hand experience and an affinity with livestock or machinery. Is the implication that the girls needed to follow the academic route in order to succeed in the STEM economy? Are these plot-lines exemplifying the accepted idea that 'girls' achievement was attributed to their plodding diligence and 'hard work' whereas boys' lower achievements were explained as due to a lack of application' (Archer et al., 2013, p. 185)? *The Archers*' males don't need to study STEM subjects, they can just do it?

With or without science qualifications, the young adults in Ambridge, regularly investigate new cropping plans, breeding regimes and production ideas data are systematically collected and discussed and Tom Archer's Nuffield scholarship has focussed attention on the need to (reluctantly) analyse and communicate findings. The scientific method is alive and well in Ambridge. The word 'research' is used regularly, but interestingly 'scientific' is never used as a term to describe either process or content. This is despite the activity of gathering evidence to empirically test ideas about the natural and material world being a regular part of professional life in Ambridge for both men and women. Gender does not appear to affect agency or identity in terms of 'working scientifically',

disputing research that argues that 'the underpinning constructions of science careers as "clever", "brainy", "not
nurturing" and "geeky" sit in opposition to the girls' self-
identification as "normal", "girly", "caring" and "active"'
(Archer et al., 2013, p. 187). We don't know whether Susan
has an O Level in chemistry but a fear of being a 'geek' didn't
appear to affect her confidence to hypothesise and conduct
scientific trials in the field of fermentation when she aspired to
the kefir manager post.

SCIENCE CAPITAL

A useful tool to help analyse why a high proportion of women
in Ambridge see science as for them is the concept of science
capital, developed by the Enterprising Science team, a five-
year partnership between King's College London and the
Science Museum (and funded by BP), and drawn from the
sociologist Pierre Bourdieu's concept of capital, referring to
economic, cultural and social resources:

> The concept of science capital can be imagined like a
> holdall, or bag, containing all the science-related
> knowledge, attitudes, experiences and resources that
> you acquire through life. It includes what science you
> know, how you think about science (your attitudes
> and dispositions), who you know (e.g. if your
> parents are very interested in science) and what
> sort of everyday engagement you have with science
> *(Archer et al., 2016, p. 2).*

Research evidence shows that young people with high
science capital are more likely to aspire to continue with
science post-16 and to see themselves as having a science
identity; but that only 5% of young people have high science

capital (Archer et al., 2016, p. 3). Science capital is a complex concept. While recognising the importance of qualitatively understanding the ways in which science capital 'works' in practice, a 'quick and dirty' approximation of the science capital of the young employed people in *The Archers*, based on information available to the long-time listener, helps us to reflect on why there are proportionally high numbers of successful female STEM professionals in the village. It may also offer useful guidance to ensure that Kiera and Poppy Grundy, as well as George Grundy, Henry and Jack Archer fulfil their potential in STEM. The analysis, presented in table 12.1, uses the four key dimensions Archer describes as being included in a young person's science capital holdall, but as relatively little is shared about children and teenagers' everyday lives in *The Archers*, engagement with extracurricular science through visits to aquaria, science centres or museums, or via TV programmes, books or the Internet cannot be included in this analysis. However, this rough and partial analysis indicates that levels of science capital are relatively high within the community, and that all of the young people surveyed, apart from Daniel Hebden Lloyd, are employed in areas that can be loosely classified as STEM, although there are role models for many non-STEM occupations in the village. Can the two data sets, high levels of science capital and STEM employment, be linked?

Archer et al. (2016, p. 4) acknowledge that 'science capital is an important factor influencing science aspirations and participation in science, but is not the only factor and it does not operate in isolation'. In *The Archers* a positive attitude towards agricultural science is invested with other weighty and regularly promoted values such as belonging, stewardship, nurture and status. It would be naive to assume that the advantages of the children of landowning families have not informed their career choices. There is no doubt that the

Jane Turner and Clare Warren

Table 12.1 Analysis of Estimated Science Capital of Employed Characters Aged Under 40 in *The Archers* Who Have Featured in the Programme During Their Childhood, Ranked From High to Low.

HIGH ← SCIENCE CAPITAL

Science Capital Indicators From Childhood	What Science You Know	How You Think About Science	Who You Know Who Works in Science	What Sort of Everyday Engagement You Have With Science	Now Employed as
Alice Carter	M Level	Very positive in academic and hands on sense, saw potential to diversify, confident to apply for engineering	1 parent + extended family, married to farrier	Grew up on farm, helped at fishing lake and riding course, keen rider	Engineer
Pip Archer	BSc	Very positive in academic and hands on sense, within traditional farming career path. Research-led approach	2 parents + extended family	Grew up on farm, helped out, attended Young Farmers	Farmer
Tom Archer	Tertiary qualification?	Motivated by business side, will engage with academic study, sees transferability of science into other areas	2 parents + extended family	Grew up on farm, took over pork production from brother	Farmer/food producer
Helen Archer	Unknown	Bought into family organic mission, inventive	2 parents + extended family	Grew up on farm, helped in dairy	Cheese maker
Josh Archer	A Levels subjects unknown	Motivated by commercial aspect rejects academic science, sees transferability of science into other areas	2 parents + extended family	Grew up on farm, helped out, beekeeping	Farmer, mechanic, dealer
Chris Carter	Apprenticeship	Made positive choices to pursue trade, rejected academic route	1 parent farming, 1 in dairy work, married to engineer	Father kept pigs, helped out	Farrier

LOW →

Name					
Will Grundy	Apprenticeship	Happiest working on the land	1 parent farming, 1 in dairy work + grandparent	Grew up on farm and helped out, learnt country skills	Game keeper
Johnny Phillips	Tertiary qualification	Proud of his farmer dad, interested, affinity with stock	Grandparents, aunt and uncle	Grew up on farm from age 16, helped with stock	Agricultural apprentice
Jamie Perks	GCSE	Made positive choices to pursue trade, rejected academic route	Neighbours	Grew up in pub in rural village	Tree surgeon
Ed Grundy	No qualifications	Only ever considered farm work	1 parent farming, 1 in dairy work + grandparent	Grew up on farm, helped out	Contractor
Emma Grundy	No qualifications	Positive about breeding potential, prepared to get hands dirty	1 parent farming, 1 in dairy work	Father kept pigs, didn't get involved	Production line/cleaner/catering
Daniel Hebden Lloyd	Humanities A Levels	Astronomy interest as a child	1 parent + extended family	Grew up with veterinary practice and stables	Soldier
Jazzer McCreary	No qualifications	Loves his 'girls'	Unknown	Unknown	Pig man
Rex Fairbrother	Unknown	Enjoying animal husbandry, very positive about becoming a farmer, land-owing family	Unknown	Unknown	Pig man/taxi driver
Toby Fairbrother	Unknown	Motivated by commercial aspect, sees entrepreneurial potential, land-owing family	Unknown	Unknown	Distiller

Ambridge young people with higher levels of science capital come from the wealthier families, and it is these young people whose STEM careers are progressing most rapidly. This supports Archer's findings that on the whole, students with high science capital are more likely to come from socially advantaged backgrounds (Archer et al., 2016). It would be unrealistic to assume that Pip and Alice have not encountered the equity, access, curriculum and identity barriers preventing females entering STEM careers that are reported elsewhere in the UK (WISE, 2018). But, from a listener's perceptive, they appear to have overcome them quite easily. What can policymakers learn from their success, and that of the other women, Susan, Clarrie, Hannah, Helen, Debbie, Pat, Ruth and even Lexi and Emma who earn their living in STEM occupations? Are their career choices evidence of a community where science capital is high? What might the rest of the UK learn from the Ambridge Women's STEM bubble?

Ways to increase students' Science Capital are being developed and tested at the time of writing (Archer, DeWitt, & King, 2018). Perhaps *The Archers*, already a community with high levels of science capital, should become a test bed for such initiatives. Could Justin Elliot be persuaded to include a new science park in his next development plans? This might bring some new residents to Ambridge who pursue non – agricultural STEM careers. Might Alice volunteer as a STEM Ambassador to work with local youth groups and schools? Will Linda get the village involved in the Great Science Share (Great Science Share, 2019)? Could the words 'science', 'technology', 'engineering' and 'maths' be entered into the script as frequently as 'business' and 'cake'? Science is everywhere in Ambridge; and everyone needs to think it is for them, if *The Archers* is going to continue to play its part in keeping the STEM pipeline flowing.

REFERENCES

Archer, L., DeWitt, J., & King, H. (2018). *Improving science participation: Five evidence-based messages for policy-makers and funders*. London: UCL Institute of Education

Archer, L., DeWitt, J., Osborne, J., Dillon, J., Willis, B., Wong, B. (2012). Balancing acts: Elementary school girls' negotiation of femininity, achievement, and science. *Science Education, 96*(6), 967–989.

Archer, L., DeWitt, J., Osborne, J., Dillon, J., Willis, B., Wong, B. (2013). Not girly, not sexy, not glamorous': Primary school girls' and parents' constructions of science aspirations. *Pedagogy, Culture and Society, 21*(1), 171–194.

Archer, L., et al (2016). *Science capital made clear*. Retrieved from https://kclpure.kcl.ac.uk/portal/en/publications/science-capital-made-clear. Accessed on 23 August 2018.

Confederation of British Industry. (2015). *Tomorrow's world inspiring primary scientists*. London: CBI. Retrieved from http://www.cbi.org.uk/tomorrows-world/assets/download. pdf. Accessed on 23 August 2018.

Frith, C., Arnot, S. (2010). The Archers Archive. BBC Books.

Gillard, D. (2018). *Jim Callaghan – Ruskin College speech (1976)*. Educationengland.org.uk. Retrieved from http://www.educationengland.org.uk/documents/speeches/1976 ruskin.html. Accessed on 23 August 2018.

Great Science Share. 2019. *Home*. Retrieved from https://www.greatscienceshare.org/. Accessed on 23 August 2018.

Hendy, D. (2007). *Life on air: A history of radio four*. Oxford: Oxford University Press.

House of Lords: Select Committee on Science and Technology. (2018). *2nd report of session 2012–13 higher education in science, technology, engineering and mathematics (STEM) subjects.* London: House of Lords.

National Audit Office. (2018). *Delivering STEM (science, technology, engineering and mathematics) skills for the economy.* London: National Audit Office

Stem.org.uk. (2018). *Skills shortage costing STEM sector £1.5bn.* Retrieved from https://www.stem.org.uk/news-and-views/news/skills-shortage-costing-stem-sector-15bn. Accessed on 23 August 2018.

Whitelegg, E. (2015). Gender and science learning. Update to block 4 In *Contemporary issues in science education.* Milton Keynes: The Open University.

WISE. (2018). *Women in STEM Workforce 2017 Welcome to the WISE Campaign'.* Available from https://www.wise-campaign.org.uk/statistics-category/workforce/. Accessed on 23 August 2018.

13

I AM WOMAN HEAR ME ROAR – AND NOW WATCH ME PLAY CRICKET

Katharine Hoskyn

ABSTRACT

Women roared into the Ambridge Cricket Team in March 2017. Their debut was initiated by a shortage of male players and a belief that the team was at risk, rather than an inherent desire to include women in the game. The approach of the women very much reflected the sentiments of the Helen Reddy 'I am Woman' song of the 1970s, 'I am woman, hear me roar in numbers too big to ignore', which became an anthem for empowerment of women in that generation. This chapter describes the context of cricket and sport in England and a synopsis of the 2017 storyline surrounding the Ambridge Cricket Team. A comparison of the storyline with the wider context shows the experience in Ambridge is similar to other places in England and elsewhere.

ENGLISH CRICKET

For centuries the organisation of sport has been based on gender, with men's and women's sport historically governed by different organisations, and the male game having the dominant profile (Osborne & Skillen, 2010, p. 190; Velija, Ratna, & Flintoff, 2014, p. 212). Towards the end of the twentieth century, funding bodies and national sporting organisations made it clear that gender equity was expected, and men's and women's associations in most sports started to merge, both internationally and nationally. At local level in England, the decision was (and still is) left to individual clubs. However, most major funding bodies require a sports organisation to demonstrate support for gender equity as a pre-requisite to receipt of financial assistance. The merging of the men's and women's national governing bodies for the English cricket occurred in 1998. This merger arose from financial difficulties experienced by the Women's Cricket Association and required more than one AGM of the women's organisation to pass (Velija Ratna, and Flintoff, 2014, p. 213). Separate competitions were, and in many sports still are, held for males and females. This differentiation is now being questioned in many quarters (Osborne & Skillen, 2010, p. 194). The main rationale given for separating men's and women's sport was the differing physique and strength of men compared with women. However, in cricket the problem is more deep-seated. Historically, cricket was regarded as an unladylike or inappropriate sport for women (Davies, 2008, p. 289; Nicholson, 2012, p. 771; Ryan, 2016, p. 2,124). Many of those attitudes still exist (Velija & Malcolm, 2009, p. 639). Men's sport has traditionally held the high ground (Lusted & Fielding-Lloyd, 2017, p. 54; Osborne & Skillen, 2010, p. 189; Velija, 2015, p. 3). The men's sport has higher profile and is regarded as the mainstay, with the women's game as the alternative. For example, in cricket there is The Cricket World Cup and The Ashes, with the women's competitions named diminutively and pejoratively as The Women's Cricket World Cup and The Women's Ashes. This is particularly interesting for cricket with the inaugural Women's Cricket World Cup being held in 1973 (Duncan, 2013, p. 5), pre-dating the men's competition by two years (Velija, 2015, p. 97).

In England, women have been very successful at cricket, and the women have an increasing, albeit still a lower, profile than the men. The women's game receives lower attention from broadcasters, academics and audiences (Velija, 2015, p. 3; Williams, 2011, p. 164). Many of the advances in the treatment of women cricketers are credited to Rachael Heyhoe Flint, a former high-profile cricketer and captain of England from 1966 to 1978, who successfully advocated for the English women's cricket team to be salaried professionals with a year-round itinerary and similar support as their male counterparts (Whitehead, 2017). Women's cricket has a longstanding and illustrious history in England and Wales (Duncan, 2013, p. 4). The first recorded match for women in village cricket is as early as 1745 (Velija, 2015, p. 25). The women's national governing body was formed in 1926 and became a founder member of the International Women's Cricket Council in 1958 (Velija, 2015, p. 7). The women's game contributed significantly to the sport both historically and recently. The England Women's Cricket team (which covers England and Wales) has won the Women's Cricket World Cup four times, an achievement completely eluding their male counterparts to date.

There is a distinction between women's cricket and women in cricket. The first refers to an all-women's team playing in competitions with other similar teams. The latter describes females playing cricket with males and is the scenario that applies to the Ambridge cricket team. The latter is often described as women joining or playing in a men's team, rather than a mixed team of players. English Cricket Board guidelines allow girls or women to participate in otherwise all-boy leagues. Yet, 'it should be noted, however, that the underlying tenor of these guidelines is not so much designed to treat sex as an irrelevant category for participation, but to make provision for a limited number of suitably talented girls to play in what will essentially remain a "boys" team' (Velija & Malcolm, 2009, p. 633). The difficulties of integrating women into men's clubs are well documented (Lusted & Fielding-Lloyd, 2017, p. 61).

High-profile media coverage in the lead-up to the Ambridge story came not from cricket but from golf. The St Andrews Golf Club admitted women in 2014 after considerable discussion and years of intense criticism. The club found the decision had unexpected implications. More than two years later, considerable publicity surrounded a perception of inequity in the changing facilities at the club. Another Scottish club, the Muirfield Golf Club, voted in 2016 to continue its male-only tradition and thus lost the right to host significant golf tournaments. A further vote on admission of women was scheduled for early 2017. The media coverage of both these cases drew attention to the issue of admission of women to male clubs (Murray, 2017).

THE AMBRIDGE STORY

It may appear that the Ambridge team is behind the times, rather like the high-profile golf clubs. The club has previously discussed the issue of admission of women to the team and shown resistance to change. Opportunity arose in 2012 when Natalie, a friend of team member Jamie Perks, wanted to join him in playing cricket. The captain of the day, Alistair Lloyd, was startled as he had never considered that a girl or woman would want to play in the Ambridge team. As explained in the programme summary, 'Natalie takes the opportunity to ask Alistair why girls can't be considered for the regular team. Alistair promises to raise it at the next AGM. Natalie is hopeful the Ambridge cricket team will soon reflect a twenty-first century ethos' (BBC, 2012). Five years later Natalie's wish had still not come to fruition. In February 2017 Alistair counsels the current coach, Harrison Burns, that an Ambridge Cricket Club AGM had discussed the possibility of women in the team previously and that it has been voted down (BBC, 2017a).

A synopsis of the recent storyline is that Harrison Burns as coach had increasing difficulty in fielding an all-male cricket team for matches against local villages. A general meeting turns down his first suggestion of admitting women to the team. At the second attempt, Harrison re-presents the case, suggesting that admission of women is the only solution. The suggestion is hotly debated, with the argument tending to be against the idea. Harrison then presents an alternative solution of a possible merger with the Darrington team, with a false comment about an email from its captain. The meeting then agrees to admit women (BBC, 2017b). Individual women are 'invited' to try out for the team based on Harrison's perception of their likely interest and talent in playing cricket. In conversation with Harrison, Usha Franks, one of the older generation, voices her question of why she was not approached to try out. Harrison implies that her age is the reason she had not been invited. The women of Ambridge are offended about Harrison's 'invitation' process and are vocal in their criticism. Younger women boycott cricket practice in protest. Harrison relents and takes a more inclusive approach to trials for the team. The trials for women players produce the usual range of possibilities. Firstly, Usha is an interested woman who is not good at the game, in her own words, she is 'rubbish'. The discussion about this situation is a difficult and painful process for both Usha and Harrison. Secondly, there are interested women who are very good at the game such as Lily Pargetter, Anisha Jayakody, Molly Button and Tracy Horrobin. Thirdly, Susan Carter is a good player but not interested in playing regularly. Susan was a pivotal woman in organising the protest against Harrison's women player assumptions. Having made her point and proving her natural cricketing skill, and with honour thus restored, Susan had no hesitation in communicating her lack of interest to Harrison. Following team selection, Harrison's difficulties continue. The inexperienced women cause havoc at 'nets' (practice sessions); selection for individual matches is difficult; and there are problems arranging appropriate changing facilities. The women all enthusiastically attend nets, at which their inexperience tests the patience of both Harrison and the experienced players. With the problems at practices and a negative attitude to female players, an experienced player, Will Grundy, decides not to attend. Harrison then selects players for matches based on attendance at nets. Will missed out on selection and complains. This omission of a talented long-standing player causes controversy amongst the other men. Further issues occur due to shared changing facilities, with the men and women separated only by a curtain across the middle of the room.

ISSUES AND PARALLELS

The storyline in *The Archers* takes an interpretative approach. The programme carefully and diligently unfolds the perspective of each person or group involved in the situation. An interpretative approach gives the perspective of participants, so that each position can be fully understood (Grant & Giddings, 2002, p. 17). The perspectives covered are Harrison as coach, the women, the men in favour of women players and the men against women players. Each perspective is portrayed to give full understanding of the views and emotions as experienced by each character without judgement of their stance. The coach seemed to have the best interests of the team at heart and clearly found the role stressful. He made some unusual decisions, seemingly a good idea at the time, which he later regretted. Harrison reflects well the difficult position of the coach of a community team. He has the role, largely because no one else will undertake the job. He has no training as a sport coach and is doing his best. Harrison's initial selection of women was based on his assessment about interest and talent. His assessment turned out to be accurate, but he made the mistake of making assumptions rather than involving the women (and maybe the men as well) in the decision-making. At times he feels he has no friends, with women vocal in their criticism of his efforts and division amongst the men.

The women are initially excited about the prospect of playing for or seeing women in the Ambridge Cricket Team. They are enraged at the ageism they perceive in Harrison's actions and are vocal in their comments to and about him. They collectively support women they perceive to be unfairly treated. In general, the women were more united than the men. This is not atypical in a sports club in which women are the minority. The men are divided on almost every issue. Some support Harrison throughout the process, even during the revelation of his telling a lie at the AGM. Others are critical of everything he does. Will is not included in the team for a match based on his non-attendance at practices and is hurt that his past loyalty seems to have been discounted. The men supporting Will do not engage in the boycotting measures of the women when one of their own is excluded. The arguments between the men demonstrate the differing opinions of cricket club members who support change and those who do not, as occurs in many sport clubs not only in England but worldwide.

CONCLUDING NOTE

As with the Ambridge cricket team, many sports clubs admitted women for reasons other than an inherent desire for gender equity. The local Ambridge cricket team had a similar experience to many of these clubs, including the prestigious St Andrews Golf Club, in finding unexpected implications in admitting women to a previously all-male environment and the changing facilities were a high-profile problem. As can be found in many local sports teams, the coach is a well-intentioned keen amateur, who has often inherited the role and its associated problems with little experience or training to deal with the issues of coaching an amateur side. Division in the club is experienced in the process. However, unlike many sports clubs, some issues were conveniently resolved quickly. Interestingly, the solutions for two of these issues in Ambridge were provided by women. Harrison's handling of the AGM is eventually exposed by Will who decides not to pursue the matter, due to the passing of Caroline Sterling, a good family friend. Changing facilities for women are purchased with a donation by Christine Barford. The issues relating to the integration of women into a men's team would usually continue for some months or even years. In a programme that covers the wide-ranging life of a village, the issues will no doubt emerge from time to time, when the storyline again focusses on the Ambridge cricket team. The team seems to live from one match to the next, with little succession planning and so further issues are likely to arise. The women of Ambridge proved their worth in a match against Netherfield in mid-2017, and this success continues into 2018. In the same way, success for women's cricket in England and Wales continued through 2017, culminating with England again winning the Cricket Women's World Cup. It is almost certainly a coincidence that this storyline occurred shortly after the death in January 2017 of Rachael Heyhoe Flint, a leading advocate for women in cricket. The storyline in Ambridge would have been well underway by this time. However, it is perhaps a fitting tribute to her that the Ambridge team admitted women in March 2017.

REFERENCES

BBC. (2012, February 17). *The Archers*. Retrieved from https://www.bbc.co.uk/programmes/b01ks5xp. Accessed 27 October 2018.

BBC. (2017a, February 15). *The Archers*. Retrieved from https://www.bbc.co.uk/programmes/b08dnwrt. Accessed 27 October 2018.

BBC. (2017b, March 09). *The Archers*. Retrieved from https://www.bbc.co.uk/programmes/b08h08kk. Accessed 27 October 2018.

Davies, P. J. (2008). Bowling maidens over: 1931 and the beginnings of women's cricket in a Yorkshire town. *Sport in History*, *28*(2), 280–298.

Duncan, I. (2013). *Skirting the boundary.* London: The Robson Press.

Grant, B. M., & Giddings, L. S. (2002). Making sense of methodologies: A paradigm framework for the novice researcher. *Contemporary Nurse: A Journal for the Australian Nursing Profession, 13*(1), 10–28.

Lusted, J., & Fielding-Lloyd, B. (2017). The limited development of English women's recreational cricket: A critique of the liberal "absorption" approach to gender equality. *Managing Sport & Leisure, 22*(1), 54–69.

Murray, E. (2017, January 25). St Andrews women members still have no changing room in main clubhouse. *The Guardian.* Retrieved from https://www.theguardian.com/sport/blog/2017/jan/25/st-andrews-women-members-changing-rooms–clubhouse. Accessed 27 October 2018.

Nicholson, R. (2012). Who killed schoolgirl cricket? The Women's Cricket Association and the death of an opportunity, 1945–1960. *History of Education, 41*(6), 771–786.

Osborne, C. A., & Skillen, F. (2010). The state of play: Women in British sport history. *Sport in History, 30*(2), 189–195.

Ryan, G. (2016). "They came to sneer, and remained to cheer": Interpreting the 1934–35 England Women's Cricket tour to Australia and New Zealand. *The International Journal of the History of Sport, 33*(17), 2123–2138.

Velija, P. (2015). *Women's cricket and global processes: The emergence and development of women's cricket as a global game.* Basingstoke: Palgrave Macmillan.

Velija, P., & Malcolm, D. (2009). "Look, it's a girl": Cricket and gender relations in the UK. *Sport in Society*, *12*(4–5), 629–642.

Velija, P., Ratna, A., & Flintoff, A. (2014). Exclusionary power in sports organisations: The merger between the Women's Cricket Association and the England and Wales Cricket Board. *International Review for the Sociology of Sport*, *49*(2), 211–226.

Whitehead, R. (2017, January 19). Lady Heyhoe Flint obituary. *The Guardian*. Retrieved from https://www.theguardian.com/sport/2017/jan/19/lady-rachael-heyhoe-flint-obituary. Accessed 27 October 2018.

Williams, J. (2011). *Cricket and broadcasting*. Manchester: Manchester University Press.

14

SOW'S EARS AND SILK PURSES: UPCYCLING AND *THE ARCHERS*

Madeleine Lefebvre

ABSTRACT

Upcycling was introduced in The Archers *by Fallon Rogers, who created a business from selling furniture she had upcycled. The author cites other examples from* Archers *episodes: Bert Fry's egg mobile was originally an old caravan. Eddie Grundy built Lynda Snell's shepherd's hut from farmyard scrap. Josh Archer expanded his online farm equipment sales to include old items refurbished and sold for profit. Definitions of upcycling imply that the original item has become worthless. The author, however, includes examples of nostalgic value placed on relics of a bygone age and suggests a dichotomy between the values of older versus younger Ambridge residents. Upcycling can also be viewed in a metaphorical sense: Lilian Bellamy, for example, regularly upcycled herself with cosmetic assistance. The most sinister example is that of Rob Titchener, who used coercive control to upcycle Helen (then) Titchener into the image he wanted. The author concludes that while motives may take several forms, it is Fallon Rogers who consistently uses both creativity and business sense in her upcycling endeavours.*

INTRODUCTION

The origin of the environmental movement is often traced back to the need for 'making do' and wasting nothing during World War II. In the early 1970s Earth Day was founded in the US, and Gary Anderson of the University of Southern California designed the Möbius loop of arrows now used widely to denote recycling. The three R's slogan, reduce, reuse and recycle, was born. These three R's have now expanded to six: reduce, reuse, recycle, rethink, refuse and repair. They don't include the word upcycling, but another term for upcycling is 'creative reuse'. The *Oxford Living Dictionaries* attribute the verb 'to upcycle' to the 1990s, and define it as 'the reuse of discarded objects or material in such a way as to create a product of higher quality or value than the original' (Oxford Dictionaries, n.d.). Wikipedia defines upcycling as 'the process of transforming by-products, waste materials, useless or unwanted products into new materials or products of better quality or for better environmental value' (Wikipedia, n.d.). Perhaps Urban Dictionary's least sarcastic definition among several offered by its contributors is 'the action of making a worthless object into a new one with more value' (Urban Dictionary, 2007).

Eschner (2017) wrote that the term upcycling was first used by McDonough and Braungart in their 2002 book,

Cradle to Cradle. Upcycling theory has become an academic discipline as a branch of the sustainability movement. *The Palgrave Handbook of Sustainability* (2018), for example, includes a chapter called 'Emerging Social Movements for Sustainability: Understanding and Scaling Up Upcycling in the UK'. An example of an academic researcher in this discipline is Dr Kyungeun Sung, of De Montfort University's School of Design, who notes her expertise in 'sustainable production and consumption by upcycling' (De Montfort University, n.d.). She has written numerous articles, conference presentations and book chapters. Television channels are full of programmes about making money from old items. An early programme was *The Antiques Roadshow* where items are valued by experts, but this trend has diversified into advice on making money from adapting throwaways. Two examples are BBC's *Money for Nothing*, and Channel 4's *Kirstie's Fill Your House for Free*. Rebecca Burn-Callandar (2015), writing in *The Telegraph*, noted the burgeoning popularity of upcycling. The Internet age has made commerce from upcycling very straightforward, as evidenced by the rapidly growing Remade in Britain upcycling virtual marketplace.

The BBC describes *The Archers* as 'a contemporary drama in a rural setting'. It isn't surprising, then, that the upcycling trend has reached Ambridge. Fallon Rogers' desire to create a small business for herself led her to pick up old furniture in flea markets and restore it for profitable resale. She also gained a reputation for catering; she combined these activities into running the Bridge Farm Tea Room, furnishing it with upcycled furniture and other knick-knacks, with all items for sale. She began participating in upcycling events such as the Darrington Vintage Fair, bringing Emma Grundy, her partner in the tearoom, with her. Indeed, upcycling became the catalyst for a major storyline: it is when Nic Grundy and Joe Grundy are sorting through old items to give to Fallon for the Fair that Nic suffers a scratch which eventually leads to her death from sepsis. Thus, in one of its more cautionary storylines the BBC were perhaps warning listeners to exercise care when working with old objects and to be alert to any cuts or scratches.

There have been other examples of upcycling in *The Archers*, not confined to the women of Ambridge. Bert Fry built an egg mobile for the Fairbrothers' pastured eggs venture from an old discarded trailer found in the Brookfield barn at Hollowtree. The Milkwood Permaculture blog describes an egg mobile as 'a movable chicken house designed to house laying hens at night, who by day cluck around on open pasture' (Bradley, 2012). Bert's egg mobile was admired by Carol Tregorran who dubs it 'The Good Life meets Doctor Who' (BBC Radio 4a). A vivid description, but perhaps also a scriptwriter's nod to two very popular BBC programmes. Unfortunately, the egg mobile goes up in flames due to an arson attack, and the caravan in which the Fairbrothers have been living is 'downcycled' into what Toby Fairbrother describes as the 'hen palace' (BBC Radio 4b). Bert subsequently rebuilt the egg mobile and his upcycling talent was used again when Josh Archer persuaded him to rebuild Jill's dilapidated Brookfield hen house for Open Farm Sunday on 5 June 2016. Bert went on to transform it into a much-admired Romany caravan, which became a feature in his own garden, much to the highly competitive Lynda Snell's dismay.

It is of interest that concurrent with the egg mobile development was Eddie Grundy's commission from Lynda to build a shepherd's hut for her. While Bert Fry was meticulous about his project, Eddie and his father, Joe, used scrap they found lying around Grange Farm for the shepherd's hut, incurring Lynda's displeasure in the process. She refused to pay him until he made several improvements and repairs. Both the shepherd's hut and the Romany caravan were featured on open gardens day, 12 June, in celebration of the Queen's official birthday. The shepherd's hut attracted little attention, whereas even Lynda was forced to compliment Bert on his expert handiwork with the caravan. The difference in approach to the two projects echoes the contrast in quality of the end result. A quick search of Google Images reveals both artistically beautiful and ham-fistedly ugly upcycling creations. A cynical contributor to Urban Dictionary who has perhaps seen too many of the latter defined upcycling as 'making crap out of garbage. Just like Martha Stewart used to, but "original" and more pretentious' (Urban Dictionary, 2007). Eleanor Doughty (2017) wrote in *The Telegraph*: 'The allure of the shepherd's hut has even reached Ambridge ... Eddie Grundy ... is dismissive of modern shepherd's huts, which he says "mock the working man's heritage"'. Doughty also writes (with accompanying photographic evidence) that David Cameron has a shepherd's hut. Is that what inspired Lynda – a desire to keep up with the Camerons? It is unlikely that David Cameron was copying Lynda, since he stated in an interview in *The Telegraph* (Hough, 2011): '"The Archers"? I'm more of an Eastenders Man.' Lynda is also known for reading her way through the literary classics. It was a real shepherd and his hut, we are told by Corey Charlton (2015) in the Mail Online, that was the inspiration for Thomas Hardy's Gabriel Oak character in *Far from the Madding Crowd*. Even Prince George has one, a first birthday gift, which resides at his grandfather's Highgrove home (Rayner, 2015). One can imagine Lynda regaling her Ambridge Hall guests with tales of her shepherd's hut, name-dropping these three males with whom she is no doubt smitten. In another example of upcycling, Josh Archer diversified his Ambridge Farm Machinery business from selling used farm equipment on commission to

paying Rex Fairbrother a pittance to help him restore abandoned equipment to sell at a big profit.

UPCYCLING VERSUS NOSTALGIA

Is there a tension between upcycling and nostalgia? I am
reminded of Urban Dictionary's (2007) reference to the
upcycled item having more value. David Archer and Tony
Archer as well as Joe Grundy get pleasure out of contem-
plating relics of a bygone age because their worth is rooted in
the memories they evoke. Thus they could never be worthless.
David has preserved his grandfather's horse-drawn plough as
is for the pleasure it brings in reminding him of his farming
heritage. Tony Archer purchased a vintage Fordson Major
tractor and is lovingly restoring it. Josh offers to get him a
good price for it, but Tony 'insists that he's never parting with
it' (BBC Radio 4e). According to Eddie, 'Joe (Grundy) won't
feel right at Grange Farm until (his dead wife Susan's) old
mangle is back in the yard' (BBC Radio 4c). Eddie and Ed
Grundy subsequently collect it from a field as a surprise for
Joe, as they recognize its importance to him. Is there a
dichotomy between what older and younger Ambridge generations consider of value?

UPCYCLING AND PEOPLE

Does upcycling apply to people as well as objects? It would
seem so in *The Archers*. For example, Lilian Bellamy regularly
popped off to London for a Botox and filler rejuvenation. In
her initially secret affair with Justin Elliott she admitted that
'the clandestine sneaking around makes her feel young again'
(BBC Radio 4d). As their relationship grew she was concerned

that she wasn't attractive enough to keep him. But Justin describes her as 'the full package – brains and beauty' (BBC Radio 4f). After Justin's then wife Miranda's remark that she is aware of what has been going on and that Lilian 'isn't the first; Justin usually goes for younger' (BBC Radio 4g), Lilian considers that the relationship is over, but within days Justin confirms that she's the woman he wants. Soon though, he is assuming marriage, which for Lilian is an (Am)bridge too far: she enjoys the excitement of being a mistress and bolts from The Bull when he proposes. The root of Lilian's reaction appears to be a fear of getting hurt again. Even Peggy Woolley warns Justin that Lilian 'is much more fragile than she seems' (BBC Radio 4h). Her physical upcycling activities are to boost her confidence in her appearance. Her insecurity intensifies with the approach of her seventieth birthday, and she goes to some lengths to prevent Justin from discovering her true age. Just prior to her birthday, Lilian disappears to London to have some major upcycling work including a new hairstyle. At the party Justin reveals that he knows her age, and it doesn't matter. She has at last found someone who loves her for who she is. No upcycling required.

Rob Titchener, on the other hand, set about upcycling his former wife Helen Archer into the image he wanted. He made her feel worthless, but she didn't recognize that that was what he was doing. There are many examples of his upcycling behaviour. The *Oxford Dictionaries* (n.d.) definition refers to upcycling 'discarded objects'. Rob coerced Helen into discarding her clothing style, her hairstyle, her work and her friends. Once he had ensured that the essence of the old Helen was discarded apparently (to others) by her own volition, he began the upcycling process.

It is interesting to contrast the upcycling of Lilian and Helen. In both cases a new hairstyle is part of the process. Lilian chooses it to boost her self-confidence, whereas Helen's new hairstyle is part of the upcycling Rob imposes on her, another 'dowdy-ising' attack on her self-confidence. What the women have in common is that they are both trying to please their man. Helen, however, doesn't seem to doubt that Rob wants her, whereas Lilian does doubt her ability to keep Justin interested. Unfortunately, Lilian too can fall under the spell of a manipulative, dangerous man, as evidenced by her tempestuous relationship with Matt Crawford which even threatened her future with Justin.

'Snapchat dysmorphia', a term coined by Dr Tijion Esho according to an article in *The Independent* (Hosie, 2018), may be addressed in a future storyline. The term describes young people having plastic surgery to look like their Snapchat filtered image. A BBC article calls it 'a phenomenon that's worrying mental health practitioners and cosmetic surgeons' (Davies, 2018). Several of the younger inhabitants of Ambridge are members of the selfie generation, wedded to their smartphones. Perhaps one will fall victim.

THE ARCHERS AS A DRAMA

Are past storylines and characters upcycled? Carol Tregorran is a character from the past who reappeared in recent years with new connections and storylines. Do these characters change for the modern audience or is it that when actors are replaced, the new actor brings new opportunities for character development? New editors and scriptwriters have also been known to reshape characters, sometimes causing bewilderment to long-time listeners.

Is *The Archers* itself a product of upcycling? Consider Elizabeth Gaskell's (1853/2005) *Cranford*. It was initially issued in serial format in a weekly magazine from 1851 to

1853, edited by Charles Dickens, which had the cozy title of *Household Words*. Goodreads.com describes *Cranford* as:

> A portrait of the residents of an English country town …. Through a series of vignettes, Elizabeth Gaskell portrays a community governed by old-fashioned habits and dominated by friendships between women. A wry account of rural life …undercut, however, by tragedy in its depiction of such troubling events as … bankruptcy, violent death … or … cruelty *(Goodreads, n.d.)*.

The description is not far removed from *The Archers*. In the novel, Miss Matty says: 'It is very pleasant dining with a bachelor…I only hope it is not improper; so many pleasant things are!' (Gaskell, 1853/2005, p. 43). I can hear Jill Archer saying that, punctuated with her delightful giggle. *Cranford* itself has been upcycled into a TV series with Dame Judi Dench in the role of Miss Matty. It was filmed in the Wiltshire village of Lacock, a name with the same two syllable stress as Cranford, and indeed Ambridge. A coincidence? Consider this: in her autobiography, talking about the TV series, Dench (2014, p. 206) describes a scene:

> … the carriage came round the corner, and we had to come out of the cottage, when Eileen had to say 'Welcome to Cranford'… They said: 'Action, Eileen and Judi', so we went out and Eileen said: Welcome to Ambridge.

FINAL OBSERVATIONS

Of the men of Ambridge, Bert Fry comes the closest in terms of creating something better from something worthless. He is a craftsman who takes pride in his work for its own sake, often for the benefit of his neighbours. Eddie Grundy, on the other hand, settles for a 'good enough' approach. The Archer cousins, Tony and David, both see intrinsic value in a relic of the past. Josh Archer seeks monetary gain from upgrading farm equipment, with little interest in the item itself. Of the women, it was Fallon Rogers who introduced the concept of upcycling proper. She has created a business from it but also takes pleasure in the actual work. As a character she has steadily grown over the years into a responsible, level-headed and industrious entrepreneur, displaying both left brain and right brain talents. I see no reason why she won't continue to diversify and expand her entrepreneurial activities. She may be a future Borsetshire Business Person of the Year. Fallon is definitely on the upcycle.

REFERENCES

BBC Radio 4(a). (2016, March 13). *The Archers*. Retrieved from https://www.bbc.co.uk/programmes/b073656g. Accessed on 28 October 2018.

BBC Radio 4(b). (2016, March 22). *The Archers*. Retrieved from https://bbc.co.uk/programmes/b0742hlc. Accessed on 28 October 2018.

BBC Radio 4(c). (2016, October 11). *The Archers*. Retrieved from https://www.bbc.co.uk/programmes/b07x2zp6. Accessed on 28 October 2018.

BBC Radio 4(d). (2017, January 31). *The Archers*. Retrieved from https://www.bbc.co.uk/programmes/b08bzj51. Accessed on 28 October 2018.

BBC Radio 4(e). (2017, February 7). *The Archers*. Retrieved from https://www.bbc.co.uk/programmes/b08crzr9. Accessed on 28 October 2018.

BBC Radio 4(f). (2017, February 24). *The Archers*. Retrieved from https://www.bbc.co.uk/programmes/b08fdbd5. Accessed on 28 October 2018.

BBC Radio 4(g). (2017, March 6). *The Archers*. Retrieved from https://www.bbc.co.uk/programmes/b08gwy5n. Accessed on 28 October 2018.

BBC Radio 4(h). (2017, April 3). *The Archers*. Retrieved from https://www.bbc.co.uk/programmes/b08ktvb8. Accessed on 28 October 2018.

Bradley, K. (2012, April 18). Egg mobiles I have loved. *Milkwood Permaculture blog*. Retrieved from https://www.milkwood.net/2012/04/18/egg-mobiles-i-have-loved/. Accessed on 28 October 2018.

Burn-Callandar, R. (2015, May 21). The 1200 pounds desk made from junk: how'upcycling' became the hot new industry. *The Telegraph*. Retrieved from https://www.telegraph.co.uk/finance/yourbusiness/11621425/The-1200-desk-made-from-junk-how-upcycling-became-the-hot-new-craft-industry.html. Accessed on 28 October 2018.

Charlton, C. (2015, April 30). Shepherd's hut used by the man who helped inspire Thomas Hardy's Far from the Madding Crowd is fully restored after being found rotting in a hedge. *DailyMail.com*. Retrieved from http://www.dailymail.co.uk/news/article-3062445/Shepherd-s-hut-used-man-helped-inspire-Thomas-Hardy-s-Far-Madding-Crowd-fully-restored-rotting-hedge.html. Accessed on 28 October 2018.

Davies, A. (2018, May 19). People are getting surgery to look like their Snapchat selfies. *BBC 3*. Retrieved from https://www.bbc.co.uk/bbcthree/article/9ca4f7c6-d2c3-4e25-862c-03aed9ec1082. Accessed on 28 October 2018.

DeMontfort University. (n.d.). *About DMU: A full listing of academic staff*. Retrieved from http://www.dmu.ac.uk/about-dmu/academic-staff/art-design-humanities/kyungeun-sung/kyungeun-sung.aspx. Accessed on 28 October 2018.

Dench, J. (2014). *Behind the scenes*. New York, NY: St. Martin's Press.

Doughty, E. (2017, May 1). Gardening: How the shepherd's hut became the new middle-class must-have. *The Telegraph*. Retrieved from http://www.telegraph.co.uk/gardening/tools-and-accessories/shepherds-hut-became-new-middle-class-must-have/. Accessed on 28 October 2018.

Eschner, K. (2017, February 21). The inventors of upcycling published their manifesto in a plastic book: Why?. *TheSmithsonian.com*. Retrieved from https://www.smithsonianmag.com/smart-news/inventors-upcycling-published-their-idea-plastic-book-why-180962182/. Accessed on 28 October 2018.

Gaskell, E. (1853/2005). *Cranford* (Penguin Classics Edition). London: Penguin Group.

Goodreads. (n.d.). *Cranford*. Retrieved from Goodreads: https://www.goodreads.com/book/show/182381.Cranford?from_search=true. Accessed on 28 October 2018.

Hosie, R. (2018, February 6). More people want surgery to look like a filtered version of themselves. *Independent.co.uk*. Retrieved from https://www.independent.co.uk/life-style/cosmetic-surgery-snapchat-instagram-filters-demand-celebrities-doctor-dr-esho-london-a8197001.html. [Accessed on 28 October 2018].

Hough, A. (2011, December 5). David Cameron: 'The Archers?' I'm more of an Eastenders man. *The Telegraph*.

Retrieved from https://www.telegraph.co.uk/news/politics/
david-cameron/8934091/David-Cameron-The-Archers-Im-
more-of-an-EastEnders-man.html. Accessed on 28 October
2018.

Oxford Dictionaries. (n.d.). *Oxford living dictionaries*.
Retrieved from https://en.oxforddictionaries.com/defini-
tion/upcycle. Accessed on 28 October 2018.

Rayner, G. (2015, July 28). Prince George's birthday present
revealed – and it's a whopper. Retrieved from https://www.
telegraph.com.uk/news/uknews/prince-george/11768995/
Prince-Georges-birthday-present-revealed-and-its-a-whopper.
html. Accessed on October 2018.

Urban Dictionary. (2007). *Upcycling*. Retrieved from https://
www.urbandictionary.com/define.php?term=Upcycling&
defid=2678724. Accessed on 28 October 2018.

Wikipedia. (n.d.). *Upcycling*. Retrieved from Wikipedia:
https://en.wikipedia.org/wiki/Upcycling.

INDEX OF AMBRIDGE RESIDENTS

Aldridge, Brian, 12, 51, 57,
        67, 78
    Debbie, 17, 108,
        156
    Jennifer, 14, 70, 103,
        128, 148
    Kate, 67, 103
    Phoebe, 17, 71, 73,
        103
Archer, Ben, 67
    David, 19, 56, 184
    Helen, 13, 16, 29, 30,
        44, 57, 59, 71,
        103–105, 136–138,
        156, 185
    Henry, 28, 67
    Jack, 161
    Jill , 70, 90, 92, 148,
        182, 187
    John, 16
    Josh, 67, 159, 179, 182,
        183, 184
    Kenton, 90, 91, 93
    Pat, 16, 70, 132, 148,
        156
    Pip, 56, 67, 71, 73, 79,
        105–106
    Rosie, 103

    Ruth (Pritchard), 17, 67,
        71, 73, 156, 158,
        164
    Tom, 44, 59, 103, 159
    Tony, 184, 188
Archie, 79

Bamford, Justin, 80
Barford, Christine, 73,
        175
Bellamy, Lilian, 57, 73,
        179, 184
Blocker, Paul 'Fat Paul',
        80
Booth, Nathan, 80
Booth, Neville, 80
Burns, PC Harrison, 171
Button, Molly, 81, 172
Button, Tilly, 80

Carter, Alice (Aldridge),
        72
Carter, Neil, 38
Carter, Susan (Horrobin),
        3, 5, 21–32, 37, 38,
        82, 147
Craig, Ian, 148
Crawford, Matt, 56, 186

Donovan, Ruairi, 12, 67
Drexler, Evan, 79
E
Elliot, Justin, 24, 79, 164

Fairbrother, Rex, 184
    Toby, 105, 182
Franks, Usha, 71, 171, 172
Fraser, Cameron, 107–108
Fry, Bert, 83, 179, 182,
    187–188
    Freda, 77–84

Grundy, Clarrie, 43, 57,
    156
    Eddie, 51, 57, 79, 179,
    182, 183, 188
    Emma, 17, 71, 125, 154,
    181
    George, 161
    Joe, 78, 182, 184
    Kiera, 154, 161
    Nic, 72, 182
    Poppy, 161
    Will, 74, 124, 148, 154,
    172

Hebden, Mark, 108
Hebden Lloyd, Daniel, 161
    Shula (Hebden, Archer),
    89–97, 108, 134
Holden, Becky, 80
Horrobin, Clive, 40
    Tracy, 84, 172

Jackson, Cecil , 83
Jayakody, Anisha, 55, 93,
    157, 172
Joey, 79

Lloyd, Alistair, 6, 89–97,
    191
    Prof Jim, 51, 81–82
Locke, Dr Richard, 29

Mabbott, Rosie, 80
Macy, Adam, 148
Madikane, Noluthando, 80
Makepeace, Darrell, 134
McCreary, Jack 'Jazzer', 51
Miller, Kirsty, 54, 103,
    148, 156
Moss, Phillip, 96

Odgen, Hilda (cat), 31
Olwen, 69, 70, 71, 73,
    74

Pargetter, Elizabeth
    (Archer), 27, 70, 90,
    107–109
    Lily, 172
    Nigel, 108
Perks, Jamie, 171
    Kathy, 78
Phones, Terry Two, 79
Pullen, Mr, 78

Riley, Hannah, 17, 156
    Roberta, 79
Rogers, Fallon, 69, 179,
    180, 181, 188

Scruff (dog), 73
Simmons, Barry, 80
Sintra (horse), 97
Snell, Lynda, 51, 73, 109,
    122, 127, 179, 182

Sterling, Caroline (Bone),
    108, 174

Thwaite, Richard, 80, 109
    Sabrina, 80, 109
Titchener, Rob, 13, 16, 18,
    28, 57, 82, 103, 132,
    179, 185
    Ursula, 136
Titcombe, Edgar, 80

Tregorran, Carol, 182, 186
Tucker, Bathany , 17
    Mike, 29, 106, 132
    Vicky, 106
Turner, Greg, 14, 29

Viktorova, Aleksandra
    'Lexi', 156

Woolley, Jack, 133

INDEX

Abuse, 56, 57, 137, 138
Alison Hindell
   'casualness,' 12
   circumspect, 15
   criticism, 19
   feminist, 11
   plot devices, 13
   women, role and status,
     17
'Altruism in pursuit of
   social stability,' 126
Altruistic motivations,
   121
Ambridge Cricket Team,
   173
Ambridge Farm Machinery,
   183
Ambridge support network,
   31–32
Anorexia, 136–138
The Antiques Roadshow,
   181
Archers/Bechdel–Wallace
   Test (ABW Test), 66,
   68, 69, 72
Audience survey, 144
'Auditory voyeurism,' 25
The Avengers, 66

Bechdel Test Movie List,
   68, 74
Bechdel–Wallace Test, 17,
   64–66
   female relationships, 64
   methodology, 66–67
The Bell, 97
Bible, 51
Big Society, 119
Bipolar disorder, 133
Black Panther, 147
Borsetshire Mental Health
   Trust, 29
Bridge Farm, 15, 40, 43,
   45, 73, 123
Bridge Farm Tea Room,
   181
British popular culture, 41
Brookfield cow issue, 14
Business, Energy and
   Industrial Strategy
   (BEIS), 156

Calculating conversations,
   67–70
'Casualness,' 12
Celebrity Big Brother,
   146–147

'Civil society,' 117, 118
Collective citizen action, 117
Communication studies,
        53–55
    'gestures,' 82
    gossip, 52
    non-verbal, 6, 78
*Compact Code on
        Volunteering,* 122
Confederation of British
        Industry (CBI), 155
Constituency, 17
Contraception, 106
Coronation Street, 41, 43
Cradle to Cradle, 181
Cricket, 168–170
Cricket World Cup, 169
Cultural learning, 55–56
*Custard, Culverts and
        Cake,* 116

'Depressing description,' 95
Diversity
    attitudes, 150
    gender, 144–146
Divisive character, 39–40
Divorce, 91
Down's syndrome, 106, 107
Dulle Griet, 42
Dyadic communication, 70

Eastenders, 84
Eating disorders, 134
Emerging Social
        Movements for
        Sustainability, 181
English cricket, 168–170
Environmental movement,
        180

Estimated science capital,
        162–163

'Fall of The House of
        Aldridge,' 14
Family, 94, 102, 109
Fawcett Society, 145
Female characterisation,
        64, 80
Female relationships, 64
Female representation, 74
Female writers, 22, 23
Feminine, 145
Feminisation, 22
Formal and informal power
        relations, 117–118
*Four Minutes and 33
        Seconds of Silence,*
        84
Freda's silent power, 81–84

Gay, 147
Gender, 53
    diversity, 144–146
    equality, 145
    equity, 168
    feminine, 145
    identity, 148
    masculine, 145
    and sexuality, 148
Generalised anxiety
        disorder, 133
'Gestures,' 82
Goodness of extreme
        condescension, 119
Google Images, 183
Gossips
    communication, 52

concept, 23
cultural learning, 55–56
definitions, 52
and gender, 53
health and safety
    matters, 56
'information
    superhighway,' 38
malicious, 25, 26, 52
no gossip, 58–59
origins, 23–24
person's reputation, 57
power, 44–46, 82
promiscuous, 25
sex and power, 57
social role, 23–24
untrustworthy, 54
'weaponise,' 45
Gravity, 66
Greek philosophy, 51
'Ground C,' 108
Guys and Dolls, 83

'Hardyesque country girl,'
    44
Headlam Hypothesis,
    15
Health Organisation and
    Pan American
    Health
    Organization, 104
Higher Education Statistics
    Agency, 156
High-profile media
    coverage, 170
Home Farm contamination,
    71
Homosexuality, 146

Horrobin household, 28
Hysteria, 134

'Ideally rational man,' 93
Identity
    feminine, 145
    gender, 145, 148
    masculine, 145
The Independent, 186
Informal activities, 120
'Information superhighway'
    of gossip, 38
International Women's
    Cricket Council, 169
Influence, 79, 80, 81, 83

Joint Academic Coding
    System (JACS), 156

Keeping Up Appearances,
    42
Keeping us safe, 56–57
*Kirstie's Fill Your House for
    Free,* 181

'Lady Bountiful' approach,
    120–121
The Larkins, 41
Last of the Summer Wine,
    41
Lesbian, 146
Love
    falling, 96
    good and individuals, 95
    moral philosophy, 94
    seflessness, 96
    selfishness, 96
    spiritual, 94

Madness, 135
Manipulation, 186
Marriage, 90, 92, 94
Masculine, 145
Media, 146–147
Men's sport, 169
Mental health
    definition, 29
    'real world,' 29
    significance, 30
    treatment, 29
    youth, 29
Mental health problems
    chronic, 138
    conditions, 133
    true-to-life portrayals,
        132
'Mental illness,' 30
Middle-aged woman, 41
Money for Nothing, 181
Moonlight, 147
Morals
    philosophy, 91, 93, 94
    pilgrimage, 96
    visions, 97
    vocabulary, 91, 97
Motivations/objectives, 120
Muirfield Golf Club, 170

The Name of the Rose, 66
'Narrative prostheses,' 134
National Council for
        Voluntary
        Organisations
        (NCVO), 122
Neighbourhood watch,
        37–46
Neurosis, 134

No Archers, 58–59
No gossip, 58–59

Office for National
        Statistics (ONS), 102

The Palgrave Handbook of
        Sustainability, 181
Personality disorders, 133
'Phallogocentric,' 82
Popular culture, 41
Post-traumatic stress
        disorder, 133
Power
    dynamics, 2–5
    gossip and, 44–46
    sex and, 57–58
    silent characters, 77–84
Pregnancy
    case studies, 103–109
    Down's syndrome, 107
    UK context, 101–102
    unplanned. (See
        Unplanned
        pregnancy)
'Prison camp,' 137

Quadrants, 121

Radio drama
    silent role, 79
    spoken and unspoken,
        78–79
'Realistic-ish,' 15
Recycling, 180
Right to choose, 101–109
Romeo and Juliet, 84
A Room of One's Own, 65

The Rule, 65, 73–74
Rumour, 52

Saving Private Ryan, 66
Science capital, 160–164
Science, technology,
        engineering and
        mathematics
        (STEM)
    careers, 164
    classifiers, 156
    employment, 155
    occupations, 157
    qualifications, 159
    skills gap, 154–155
Secrets, 51
Self-serving motivations,
        121
Self-starvation, 137
Separation, 90
Sex and power, 57–58
Sexuality, 144, 147
'Shared experiences and
        hopes,' 120
Silent characters
    influence, 79
    radical drama, 84
    use and function, 79–81
'Snapchat dysmorphia,'
        186
Social change, 144, 150
Social forces, 118–121
Sociocultural phenomena,
        145
Solidarity, 120
The Sovereignty of Good,
        93, 94
St Andrews Golf Club, 174

Status
    social, 24, 26, 28
    working class, 25, 26
'Steminists,' 156
'Strong woman and
        effective leader,' 12

The Telegraph, 181
Terry Two Phones, 79
Testosterone, 144
Titus Andronicus, 53
Tongue-wagging, 49–60
Transgender people, 145

Unplanned pregnancy,
        101–109
Upcycling
    'creative reuse,' 180
    vs. nostalgia, 184
    and people, 184–186
Urban Dictionary, 183
The Uses of Literacy, 41

Waiting for Godot, 84
Well-being, 28–30
Women in science, 155
Women in sport, 168, 169,
        174
Women's Ashes, 169
Women's conversations,
        63–74
Women's Cricket World
        Cup, 169
'Women's work,' 118,
        121–128
Working-class matriarch,
        40–44